EVERYDAY
RECIPES

pil

Publications International, Ltd.

Pictured on the front cover: Italian Meatball Hoagies *(page 16).*

Pictured on the back cover *(top to bottom, left to right):* Delicious Pepper Steak *(page 18),* Spinach and Ricotta Stuffed Shells *(page 38),* Mexican Carnitas *(page 68),* Ravioli Casserole *(page 96),* Parmesan Potato Wedges *(page 112),* Spaghetti Squash with Shrimp and Veggies *(page 158)* and Cauliflower Soup *(page 174).*

ISBN: 978-1-64558-207-6

Manufactured in China.

8 7 6 5 4 3 2 1

Microwave Cooking: Microwave ovens vary in wattage. Use the cooking times as guidelines and check for doneness before adding more time.

CONTENTS

SLOW COOKER SIZES

Smaller **CROCK-POT**® slow cookers—such as 1- to 3½-quart models—are the perfect size for cooking for singles, a couple or empty-nesters (and also for serving dips).

While medium-size **CROCK-POT**® slow cookers (those holding somewhere between 3 quarts and 5 quarts) will easily cook enough food at a time to feed a small family, they're also convenient for holiday side dishes or appetizers.

Large **CROCK-POT**® slow cookers are great for large family dinners, holiday entertaining and potluck suppers. A 6- to 7-quart model is ideal if you like to make meals in advance, or have dinner tonight and store leftovers for another day.

TYPES OF SLOW COOKERS

Current **CROCK-POT**® slow cookers come equipped with many different features and benefits, from auto cook programs to stovetop-safe stoneware to timed programming. Visit **WWW.CROCK-POT.COM** to find the **CROCK-POT**® slow cooker that best suits your needs.

How you plan to use a **CROCK-POT**® slow cooker may affect the model you choose to purchase. For everyday cooking, choose a size large enough to serve your family. If you plan to use the **CROCK-POT**® slow cooker primarily for entertaining, choose one of the larger sizes. Basic **CROCK-POT**® slow cookers can hold as little as 16 ounces or as much as 7 quarts. The smallest sizes are great for keeping dips warm on a buffet, while the larger sizes can more readily fit large quantities of food and larger roasts.

COOKING, STIRRING AND FOOD SAFETY

CROCK-POT® slow cookers are safe to leave unattended. The outer heating base may get hot as it cooks, but it should not pose a fire hazard. The heating element in the heating base functions at a low wattage and is safe for your countertops.

Your **CROCK-POT**® slow cooker should be filled about one-half to three-fourths full for most recipes unless otherwise instructed. Lean meats such as chicken or pork tenderloin will cook faster than meats with more connective tissue and fat such as beef chuck or pork shoulder. Bone-in meats will take longer than boneless cuts. Typical **CROCK-POT**® slow cooker dishes take approximately 7 to 8 hours to reach the simmer point on LOW and about 3 to 4 hours on HIGH. Once the vegetables and meat start to simmer and braise, their flavors will fully blend and meat will become fall-off-the-bone tender.

According to the USDA, all bacteria are killed at a temperature of 165°F. It's important to follow the recommended cooking times and not to open the lid often, especially early in the cooking process when heat is building up inside the unit. If you need to open the lid to check on your food or are adding additional ingredients, remember to allow additional cooking time if necessary to ensure food is cooked through and tender.

Large **CROCK-POT**® slow cookers, the 6- to 7-quart sizes, may benefit with a quick stir halfway through cook time to help distribute heat and promote even cooking. It's usually unnecessary to stir at all, as even ½ cup liquid will help to distribute heat, and the stoneware is the perfect medium for holding food at an even temperature throughout the cooking process.

OVEN-SAFE

All **CROCK-POT**® slow cooker removable stoneware inserts may (without their lids) be used safely in ovens at up to 400°F. Also, all **CROCK-POT**® slow cookers are microwavable without their lids. If you own another brand of slow cooker, please refer to your owner's manual for specific stoneware cooking medium tolerances.

FROZEN FOOD

Frozen food or partially frozen food can be successfully cooked in a **CROCK-POT**® slow cooker; however, it will require longer cooking time than the same recipe made with fresh food. It's almost always preferable to thaw frozen food prior to placing it in the **CROCK-POT**® slow cooker. Using an instant-read thermometer is recommended to ensure meat is fully cooked through.

PASTA AND RICE

If you're converting a recipe that calls for uncooked pasta, cook the pasta on the stovetop just until slightly tender before adding to the **CROCK-POT**® slow cooker. If you are converting a recipe that calls for cooked rice, stir in raw rice with other ingredients; add ¼ cup extra liquid per ¼ cup of raw rice.

BEANS

Beans must be softened completely before combining with sugar and/ or acidic foods. Sugar and acid have a hardening effect on beans and will prevent softening. Fully cooked canned beans may be used as a substitute for dried beans.

VEGETABLES

Root vegetables often cook more slowly than meat. Cut vegetables accordingly to cook at the same rate as meat—large versus small, or lean versus marbled—and place near the sides or bottom of the stoneware to facilitate cooking.

HERBS

Fresh herbs add flavor and color when added at the end of the cooking cycle; if added at the beginning, many fresh herbs' flavor will dissipate over long cook times. Ground and/or dried herbs and spices work well in slow cooking and may be added at the beginning, and for dishes with shorter cook times, hearty fresh herbs such as rosemary and thyme hold up well. The flavor power of all herbs and spices can vary greatly depending on their particular strength and shelf life. Use chili powders and garlic powder sparingly, as these can sometimes intensify over the long cook times. Always taste the finished dish and correct seasonings including salt and pepper.

LIQUIDS

It is not necessary to use more than ½ to 1 cup liquid in most instances since juices in meats and vegetables are retained more in slow cooking than in conventional cooking. Excess liquid can be cooked down and concentrated after slow cooking on the stovetop or by removing meat and vegetables from the stoneware, stirring in one of the following thickeners, and setting the slow cooker to HIGH. Cook on HIGH for approximately 15 minutes or until juices are thickened.

FLOUR: All-purpose flour is often used to thicken soups or stews. Stir cold water into the flour in a small bowl until smooth. With the **CROCK-POT**® slow cooker on HIGH, whisk the flour mixture into the liquid in the **CROCK-POT**® slow cooker. Cover; cook on HIGH 15 minutes or until the mixture is thickened.

CORNSTARCH: Cornstarch gives sauces a clear, shiny appearance; it's used most often for sweet dessert sauces and stir-fry sauces. Stir cold water into the cornstarch in a small bowl until the cornstarch dissolves. Quickly stir this mixture into the liquid in the **CROCK-POT**® slow cooker; the sauce will thicken as soon as the liquid boils. Cornstarch breaks down with too much heat, so never add it at the beginning of the slow cooking process, and turn off the heat as soon as the sauce thickens.

ARROWROOT: Arrowroot (or arrowroot flour) comes from the root of a tropical plant that is dried and ground to a powder; it produces a thick, clear sauce. Those who are allergic to wheat often use it in place of flour. Place arrowroot in a small bowl or cup and stir in cold water until the mixture is smooth. Quickly stir this mixture into the liquid in the **CROCK-POT**® slow cooker. Arrowroot thickens below the boiling point, so it even works well in a **CROCK-POT**® slow cooker on LOW. Too much stirring can break down an arrowroot mixture.

TAPIOCA: Tapioca is a starchy substance extracted from the root of the cassava plant. Its greatest advantage is that it withstands long cooking, making it an ideal choice for slow cooking. Add it at the beginning of cooking and you'll get a clear, thickened sauce in the finished dish. Dishes using tapioca as a thickener are best cooked on the LOW setting; tapioca may become stringy when boiled for a long time.

MILK

Milk, cream and sour cream break down during extended cooking. When possible, add them during the last 15 to 30 minutes of cooking, until just heated through. Condensed soups may be substituted for milk and can cook for extended times.

FISH

Fish is delicate and should be stirred in gently during the last 15 to 30 minutes of cooking time. Cover and cook just until cooked through and serve immediately.

BAKED GOODS

If you wish to prepare bread, cakes or pudding cakes in a **CROCK-POT**® slow cooker, you may want to purchase a covered, vented metal cake pan accessory for your **CROCK-POT**® slow cooker. You can also use any straight-sided soufflé dish or deep cake pan that will fit into the stoneware of your unit. Baked goods can be prepared directly in the stoneware; however, they can be a little difficult to remove from the insert, so follow the recipe directions carefully.

BRISKET WITH SWEET ONIONS

2 large sweet onions, cut into 10 (½-inch) slices*

1 flat-cut boneless beef brisket (about 3½ pounds)**

Salt and black pepper

2 cans (about 14 ounces *each*) beef broth

1 teaspoon cracked black peppercorns

¾ cup crumbled blue cheese (optional)

Preferably Maui, Vidalia or Walla Walla onions.

**Unless you have a 5-, 6- or 7-quart CROCK-POT® slow cooker, cut any piece of meat larger than 2½ pounds in half so it cooks completely.*

1. Coat inside of **CROCK-POT**® slow cooker with nonstick cooking spray. Line bottom with onion slices.

2. Season brisket with salt and black pepper. Heat large skillet over medium-high heat. Add brisket; cook 10 to 12 minutes or until browned on all sides. Remove to **CROCK-POT**® slow cooker.

3. Pour broth into **CROCK-POT**® slow cooker. Sprinkle brisket with peppercorns. Cover; cook on HIGH 5 to 7 hours.

4. Remove brisket to large cutting board. Cover loosely with foil; let stand 10 to 15 minutes. Slice evenly against the grain into ten slices. To serve, arrange onions on serving platter and spread slices of brisket on top. Sprinkle with blue cheese, if desired. Serve with cooking liquid.

MAKES 10 SERVINGS

HARVEST HAM SUPPER

6 medium carrots, halved and cut into 2-inch pieces

3 medium unpeeled sweet potatoes, quartered

1 to 1½ pounds boneless ham

1 cup maple syrup

Chopped fresh Italian parsley (optional)

1. Arrange carrots and potatoes in bottom of **CROCK-POT**® slow cooker. Place ham on top of vegetables. Pour maple syrup over ham and vegetables.

2. Cover; cook on LOW 6 to 8 hours. Garnish vegetables with parsley.

MAKES 6 SERVINGS

LEMON AND HERB TURKEY BREAST

1 split turkey breast
(about 3 pounds)

½ cup lemon juice

½ cup dry white wine

6 cloves garlic, minced

¼ teaspoon salt

¼ teaspoon dried parsley flakes

¼ teaspoon dried tarragon

¼ teaspoon dried rosemary

¼ teaspoon dried sage

¼ teaspoon black pepper

Sprigs fresh sage and rosemary (optional)

Lemon slices (optional)

1. Place turkey in **CROCK-POT**® slow cooker. Combine lemon juice, wine, garlic, salt, parsley flakes, tarragon, dried rosemary, dried sage and pepper in medium bowl; stir to blend. Pour lemon juice mixture over turkey in **CROCK-POT**® slow cooker.

2. Cover; cook on LOW 8 to 10 hours or on HIGH 4 to 5 hours. Garnish with fresh sage, fresh rosemary and lemon slices.

MAKES 4 SERVINGS

BASQUE CHICKEN WITH PEPPERS

1 cut-up whole chicken (about 4 pounds)

2 teaspoons salt, divided

1 teaspoon black pepper, divided

1½ tablespoons olive oil

1 onion, chopped

1 medium green bell pepper, cut into strips

1 medium yellow bell pepper, cut into strips

1 medium red bell pepper, cut into strips

8 ounces small brown mushrooms, halved

1 can (about 14 ounces) stewed tomatoes

½ cup chicken broth

½ cup Rioja wine

3 ounces tomato paste

2 cloves garlic, minced

1 sprig fresh marjoram

1 teaspoon smoked paprika

Hot cooked brown rice

4 ounces chopped prosciutto

1. Season chicken with 1 teaspoon salt and ½ teaspoon black pepper. Heat oil in large skillet over medium-high heat. Add chicken in batches; cook 6 to 8 minutes or until browned on all sides. Remove to **CROCK-POT®** slow cooker.

2. Heat same skillet over medium-low heat. Add onion; cook and stir 3 minutes or until softened. Add bell peppers and mushrooms; cook 3 minutes. Add tomatoes, broth, wine, tomato paste, garlic, marjoram, remaining 1 teaspoon salt, paprika and remaining ½ teaspoon black pepper to skillet; bring to a simmer. Simmer 3 to 4 minutes; pour over chicken in **CROCK-POT®** slow cooker.

3. Cover; cook on LOW 5 to 6 hours or on HIGH 3 to 4 hours. Serve chicken with rice. Ladle vegetables and sauce over chicken. Sprinkle with prosciutto.

MAKES 4 TO 6 SERVINGS

ITALIAN MEATBALL HOAGIES

½ **pound ground beef**

½ **pound Italian sausage, casings removed**

¼ **cup seasoned dry bread crumbs**

¼ **cup grated Parmesan cheese, plus additional for topping**

1 **egg**

1 **tablespoon olive oil**

1 **cup pasta sauce**

2 **tablespoons tomato paste**

¼ **teaspoon red pepper flakes (optional)**

4 **(6-inch) hoagie rolls, split**

1. Coat inside of **CROCK-POT®** slow cooker with nonstick cooking spray. Combine beef, sausage, bread crumbs, ¼ cup Parmesan cheese and egg in large bowl; mix well. Shape to form 12 (1½-inch) meatballs.

2. Heat oil in large skillet over medium heat. Add meatballs; cook 6 to 8 minutes or until browned on all sides, turning occasionally. Remove meatballs to **CROCK-POT®** slow cooker using slotted spoon.

3. Combine pasta sauce, tomato paste and red pepper flakes, if desired, in medium bowl; stir to blend. Spoon over meatballs; toss gently.

4. Cover; cook on LOW 5 to 7 hours or on HIGH 2½ to 3 hours. Place meatballs in rolls. Spoon sauce over meatballs; top with additional Parmesan cheese.

MAKES 4 SERVINGS

DELICIOUS PEPPER STEAK

2 tablespoons dark sesame oil

2 pounds boneless beef round steak, cut into strips

½ medium red bell pepper, sliced

½ medium green bell pepper, sliced

½ medium yellow bell pepper, sliced

1 medium onion, sliced

14 grape tomatoes

⅓ cup hoisin sauce

¼ cup water

3 tablespoons all-purpose flour

3 tablespoons soy sauce

2 teaspoons garlic powder

1 teaspoon ground cumin

1 teaspoon dried oregano

1 teaspoon paprika

⅛ teaspoon ground red pepper

Hot cooked rice (optional)

1. Heat oil in large skillet over medium-high heat. Add beef in batches; cook 4 to 5 minutes or until browned. Remove to large paper towel-lined plate.

2. Add bell peppers, onion and tomatoes to **CROCK-POT**® slow cooker. Combine hoisin sauce, water, flour, soy sauce, garlic powder, cumin, oregano, paprika and ground red pepper in medium bowl; stir to blend. Add to **CROCK-POT**® slow cooker. Add beef.

3. Cover; cook on LOW 8 to 9 hours or on HIGH 4 to 4½ hours. Serve with rice, if desired.

MAKES 8 SERVINGS

BEEFY TORTILLA PIE

2 teaspoons olive oil

1½ cups chopped onion

2 pounds ground beef

1 teaspoon chili powder

1 teaspoon ground cumin

1 teaspoon salt

2 cloves garlic, minced

1 can (15 ounces) tomato sauce

1 cup sliced black olives

7 (6-inch) flour tortillas

4 cups (16 ounces) shredded Cheddar cheese

Optional toppings: sour cream, salsa and/or chopped green onion

1. Heat oil in large skillet over medium heat. Add onion; cook and stir 3 to 5 minutes or until tender. Add ground beef, chili powder, cumin, salt and garlic; cook and stir 6 to 8 minutes or until browned. Stir in tomato sauce; heat through. Stir in black olives.

2. Prepare foil handles.* Place in **CROCK-POT**® slow cooker; spray with nonstick cooking spray. Lay one tortilla on foil strips. Spread with ⅓ of meat sauce and cheese. Repeat tortillas, meat sauce and cheese layers 6 times, ending with cheese. Cover; cook on HIGH 1½ hours.

3. Lift out of **CROCK-POT**® slow cooker using foil handles and transfer to serving platter. Discard foil. Cut into wedges. Serve with desired toppings.

Prepare foil handles by tearing off four 18X2-inch strips of heavy-duty foil (or use regular foil folded to double thickness). Crisscross foil strips in spoke design.

MAKES 4 TO 5 SERVINGS

CHICKEN MEATBALLS IN SPICY TOMATO SAUCE

3 tablespoons olive oil, divided

1 medium onion, chopped

6 cloves garlic, minced

1½ teaspoons dried basil

¼ teaspoon red pepper flakes

2 cans (about 14 ounces *each*) diced tomatoes

3 tablespoons tomato paste

2 teaspoons salt, divided

1½ pounds ground chicken

2 egg yolks

1 teaspoon dried oregano

¼ teaspoon black pepper

1. Heat 2 tablespoons oil in large skillet over medium-high heat. Add onion, garlic, basil and red pepper flakes; cook and stir 5 minutes or until onion is softened. Remove half of mixture to **CROCK-POT®** slow cooker. Stir in diced tomatoes, tomato paste and 1 teaspoon salt.

2. Remove remaining onion mixture to large bowl. Add chicken, egg yolks, oregano, remaining 1 teaspoon salt and black pepper; mix well. Form mixture into 24 (1-inch) balls.

3. Heat remaining 1 tablespoon oil in large skillet. Add meatballs in batches; cook 7 minutes or until browned. Remove to **CROCK-POT®** slow cooker using slotted spoon. Cover; cook on LOW 4 to 5 hours.

MAKES 4 SERVINGS

TURKEY MEAT LOAF

1 pound ground white meat turkey

1 pound ground dark meat turkey

1 can (about 14 ounces) diced tomatoes, drained

1 medium onion, chopped

1 medium green bell pepper, chopped

1 cup seasoned dry bread crumbs

¼ cup ketchup, plus additional for topping

2 tablespoons yellow mustard

2 eggs

2 teaspoons garlic powder

2 teaspoons dried oregano

2 teaspoons dried basil

2 teaspoons Worcestershire sauce

1 teaspoon salt

½ teaspoon black pepper

2 tablespoons packed brown sugar (optional)

1. Coat inside of **CROCK-POT**® slow cooker with nonstick cooking spray. Prepare foil handles.* Place in **CROCK-POT**® slow cooker; spray with nonstick cooking spray.

2. Combine turkey meat, tomatoes, onion, bell pepper, bread crumbs, ¼ cup ketchup, mustard, eggs, garlic powder, oregano, basil, Worcestershire sauce, salt and black pepper in large bowl; mix well. Form mixture into loaf. Place loaf on top of foil in **CROCK-POT**® slow cooker. Spread top of meat loaf with additional ketchup and brown sugar, if desired.

3. Cover; cook on LOW 7 to 8 hours or on HIGH 3½ to 4 hours. Remove meat loaf from **CROCK-POT**® slow cooker using foil handles to large cutting board. Let stand 10 minutes before slicing.

Prepare foil handles by tearing off four 18X2-inch strips of heavy-duty foil (or use regular foil folded to double thickness). Crisscross foil strips in spoke design.

MAKES 6 TO 8 SERVINGS

CROCK AND GO HAM WITH PINEAPPLE GLAZE

1 ham (3 to 5 pounds)

10 to 12 whole cloves

1 can (8 ounces) sliced pineapple, juice reserved and divided

2 tablespoons packed brown sugar

1 jar (4 ounces) maraschino cherries plus 1 tablespoon juice, reserved and divided

1. Stud ham with cloves. Place ham in **CROCK-POT**® slow cooker.

2. Combine reserved pineapple juice, brown sugar and reserved 1 tablespoon cherry juice in medium bowl; stir until glaze forms. Pour glaze over ham in **CROCK-POT**® slow cooker. Arrange sliced pineapple and cherries over ham.

3. Cover; cook on LOW 6 to 8 hours. Remove cloves before serving.

MAKES 6 TO 8 SERVINGS

CLASSIC BEEF STEW

2½ pounds cubed beef stew meat

¼ cup all-purpose flour

2 tablespoons olive oil

3 cups beef broth

16 baby carrots

8 fingerling potatoes, halved crosswise

1 medium onion, chopped

1 ounce dried oyster mushrooms, chopped

2 teaspoons garlic powder

1 teaspoon dried basil

1 teaspoon dried oregano

½ teaspoon dried rosemary

½ teaspoon dried marjoram

½ teaspoon dried sage

½ teaspoon dried thyme

Salt and black pepper (optional)

Chopped fresh Italian parsley (optional)

1. Combine beef and flour in large resealable food storage bag; toss to coat. Heat 1 tablespoon oil in large skillet over medium-high heat. Add half of beef; cook and stir 4 minutes or until browned. Remove to **CROCK-POT**® slow cooker. Repeat with remaining oil and beef.

2. Add broth, carrots, potatoes, onion, mushrooms, garlic powder, basil, oregano, rosemary, marjoram, sage and thyme to **CROCK-POT**® slow cooker; stir to blend.

3. Cover; cook on LOW 10 to 12 hours or on HIGH 5 to 6 hours. Season with salt and pepper, if desired. Garnish with parsley.

MAKES 8 SERVINGS

HAM AND SAGE STUFFED CORNISH HENS

1 cup plus 3 tablespoons sliced celery, divided

1 cup sliced leek (white part only)

2 tablespoons butter, divided

¼ cup finely diced onion

¼ cup diced smoked ham or prosciutto

1 cup seasoned stuffing mix

1 cup chicken broth

1 tablespoon finely chopped fresh sage *or* 1 teaspoon ground sage

4 Cornish hens (about 1½ pounds *each*)

Salt and black pepper

1. Coat inside of **CROCK-POT**® slow cooker with nonstick cooking spray. Toss 1 cup celery and leek in **CROCK-POT**® slow cooker.

2. Melt 1 tablespoon butter in large nonstick skillet over medium heat. Add remaining 3 tablespoons celery, onion and ham; cook and stir 5 minutes or until onion is soft. Stir in stuffing mix, broth and sage. Remove mixture to medium bowl.

3. Rinse hens and pat dry. Sprinkle inside and outside of each hen with salt and pepper. Gently spoon stuffing into cavities. Tie each hen's drumsticks together with kitchen string.

4. Melt remaining 1 tablespoon butter in same skillet over medium-high heat. Place 2 hens, breast sides down, in skillet; cook until skins brown, turning to brown all sides. Remove to **CROCK-POT**® slow cooker. Repeat with remaining hens.

5. Cover; cook on LOW 5 to 6 hours or on HIGH 3 to 4 hours. Remove string; place hens on serving platter. Spoon cooking broth over hens.

MAKES 4 SERVINGS

EASY SALISBURY STEAK

1½ pounds ground beef

1 egg

½ cup plain dry bread crumbs

1 package (about 1 ounce) dry onion soup mix*

1 can (10½ ounces) golden mushroom soup, undiluted

You may pulse onion soup mix in a small food processor or coffee grinder for a finer grind, if desired.

1. Coat inside of **CROCK-POT®** slow cooker with nonstick cooking spray. Combine beef, egg, bread crumbs and dry soup mix in large bowl. Form mixture evenly into four 1-inch thick patties.

2. Heat large skillet over medium-high heat. Add patties; cook 2 minutes per side until lightly browned. Remove to **CROCK-POT®** slow cooker, in single layer. Pour mushroom soup evenly over patties. Cover; cook on LOW 3 to 3½ hours.

MAKES 4 SERVINGS

VEGETARIAN CHILI

1 tablespoon vegetable oil

1 cup chopped onion

1 cup chopped red bell pepper

2 tablespoons minced jalapeño pepper*

1 clove garlic, minced

1 can (about 28 ounces) stewed tomatoes

1 can (about 15 ounces) black beans, rinsed and drained

1 can (about 15 ounces) chickpeas, rinsed and drained

½ cup frozen corn

¼ cup tomato paste

1 teaspoon sugar

1 teaspoon ground cumin

1 teaspoon dried basil

1 teaspoon chili powder

¼ teaspoon black pepper

Jalapeño peppers can sting and irritate the skin, so wear rubber gloves when handling peppers and do not touch your eyes.

1. Heat oil in large skillet over medium-high heat. Add onion, bell pepper, jalapeño pepper and garlic; cook and stir 5 minutes. Remove onion mixture to **CROCK-POT**® slow cooker using slotted spoon.

2. Add tomatoes, beans, chickpeas, corn, tomato paste, sugar, cumin, basil, chili powder and black pepper; stir to blend. Cover; cook on LOW 4 to 5 hours.

MAKES 4 SERVINGS

BROCCOLI AND CHEESE STRATA

4 cups water

2 cups chopped broccoli florets

4 slices firm white bread
(½ inch thick)

4 teaspoons butter

1½ cups (6 ounces) shredded
Cheddar cheese

1½ cups milk

3 eggs

½ teaspoon salt

½ teaspoon hot pepper sauce

⅛ teaspoon black pepper

1. Spray 1-quart casserole or soufflé dish that fits inside of **CROCK-POT**®
slow cooker with nonstick cooking spray. Bring water to a boil in large
saucepan; cook broccoli 10 minutes or until tender. Drain. Spread one side
of each bread slice with 1 teaspoon butter. Arrange 2 slices bread, buttered
sides up, in prepared casserole. Layer cheese, broccoli and remaining
2 bread slices, buttered sides down.

2. Whisk milk, eggs, salt, hot pepper sauce and black pepper in medium
bowl; slowly pour over bread.

3. Prepare foil handles.* Place casserole in **CROCK-POT**® slow cooker using
foil handles. Cover; cook on HIGH 3 hours.

*Prepare foil handles by tearing off four 18X2-inch strips of heavy-duty foil (or use
regular foil folded to double thickness). Crisscross foil strips in spoke design.*

MAKES 4 SERVINGS

SPINACH AND RICOTTA STUFFED SHELLS

18 uncooked jumbo pasta shells (about half of a 12-ounce package)

1 package (15 ounces) ricotta cheese

7 ounces frozen chopped spinach, thawed and squeezed dry

½ cup grated Parmesan cheese

1 egg, lightly beaten

1 clove garlic, minced

½ teaspoon salt

1 jar (24 to 26 ounces) marinara sauce

½ cup (2 ounces) shredded mozzarella cheese

1 teaspoon olive oil

1. Cook pasta shells according to package directions until almost tender. Drain well. Combine ricotta cheese, spinach, Parmesan cheese, egg, garlic and salt in medium bowl.

2. Pour ¼ cup marinara sauce in bottom of **CROCK-POT**® slow cooker. Spoon 2 to 3 tablespoons ricotta mixture into 1 pasta shell and place in bottom of **CROCK-POT**® slow cooker. Repeat with enough additional shells to cover bottom of **CROCK-POT**® slow cooker. Top with another ¼ cup marinara sauce. Repeat with remaining pasta shells and filling.

3. Top with remaining marinara sauce and sprinkle with mozzarella cheese. Drizzle with oil. Cover; cook on HIGH 3 to 4 hours or until mozzarella cheese is melted and sauce is hot and bubbly.

MAKES 6 SERVINGS

ITALIAN EGGPLANT WITH MILLET AND PEPPER STUFFING

¼ cup uncooked millet

2 small eggplants (about ¾ pound *total*), unpeeled

¼ cup chopped red bell pepper, divided

¼ cup chopped green bell pepper, divided

1 teaspoon olive oil

1 clove garlic, minced

1½ cups vegetable broth

½ teaspoon ground cumin

½ teaspoon dried oregano

⅛ teaspoon red pepper flakes

Sprigs fresh basil (optional)

1. Heat large skillet over medium heat. Add millet; cook and stir 5 minutes. Remove to small bowl; set aside. Cut eggplants lengthwise into halves. Scoop out flesh, leaving about ¼-inch-thick shell. Reserve shells; chop eggplant flesh. Combine 1 tablespoon red bell pepper and 1 tablespoon green bell pepper in small bowl; set aside.

2. Heat oil in same skillet over medium heat. Add chopped eggplant, remaining red and green bell peppers and garlic; cook and stir 8 minutes or until eggplant is tender.

3. Combine eggplant mixture, broth, cumin, oregano and red pepper flakes in **CROCK-POT**® slow cooker. Cover; cook on LOW 4½ hours or until all liquid is absorbed.

4. Turn **CROCK-POT**® slow cooker to HIGH. Fill eggplant shells with eggplant-millet mixture. Sprinkle with reserved bell peppers. Place filled shells in **CROCK-POT**® slow cooker. Cover; cook on HIGH 1½ to 2 hours. Garnish with basil.

MAKES 4 SERVINGS

CHIPOTLE VEGETABLE CHILI WITH CHOCOLATE

2 tablespoons olive oil

1 medium onion, chopped

1 medium green bell pepper, chopped

1 medium red bell pepper, chopped

1 cup frozen corn

1 can (28 ounces) diced tomatoes

1 can (about 15 ounces) black beans, rinsed and drained

1 can (about 15 ounces) pinto beans, rinsed and drained

1 tablespoon chili powder

1 teaspoon ground cumin

½ teaspoon chipotle chili powder

1 ounce semisweet chocolate, chopped

1. Heat oil in large skillet over medium-high heat. Add onion and bell peppers; cook and stir 4 minutes or until softened. Stir in corn; cook 3 minutes. Remove to **CROCK-POT**® slow cooker. Stir tomatoes, beans, chili powder, cumin and chipotle chili powder into **CROCK-POT**® slow cooker.

2. Cover; cook on LOW 6 to 7 hours. Stir chocolate into **CROCK-POT**® slow cooker until melted.

MAKES 6 SERVINGS

THAI RED CURRY WITH TOFU

1 medium sweet potato, cut into 1-inch pieces

1 small eggplant, halved lengthwise and cut crosswise into ½-inch-wide halves

8 ounces extra firm tofu, cut into 1-inch pieces

½ cup green beans, cut into 1-inch pieces

½ red bell pepper, cut into ¼-inch-wide strips

2 tablespoons vegetable oil

5 medium shallots (about 1½ cups), thinly sliced

3 tablespoons Thai red curry paste

1 teaspoon minced garlic

1 teaspoon grated ginger

1 can (about 13 ounces) unsweetened coconut milk

1½ tablespoons soy sauce

1 tablespoon packed light brown sugar

¼ cup chopped fresh basil

2 tablespoons lime juice

Hot cooked rice (optional)

1. Coat inside of **CROCK-POT**® slow cooker with nonstick cooking spray. Add potato, eggplant, tofu, beans and bell pepper.

2. Heat oil in large skillet over medium heat. Add shallots; cook 5 minutes or until browned and tender. Add curry paste, garlic and ginger; cook and stir 1 minute. Add coconut milk, soy sauce and brown sugar; bring to a simmer. Pour mixture over vegetables in **CROCK-POT**® slow cooker.

3. Cover; cook on LOW 2 to 3 hours. Stir in basil and lime juice. Serve with rice, if desired.

MAKES 4 SERVINGS

BLACK BEAN, ZUCCHINI AND CORN ENCHILADAS

1 tablespoon vegetable oil

1 medium onion, chopped

2 medium zucchini

2 cups corn

1 large red bell pepper, chopped

1 teaspoon minced garlic

½ teaspoon salt

½ teaspoon ground cumin

¼ teaspoon ground coriander

1 can (about 14 ounces) black beans, rinsed and drained

2 jars (16 ounces *each*) salsa verde

12 (6-inch) corn tortillas

2½ cups (10 ounces) shredded Monterey Jack cheese

2 tablespoons chopped fresh cilantro

1. Heat oil in large skillet over medium heat. Add onion; cook 6 minutes or until softened. Add zucchini, corn and bell pepper; cook 2 minutes. Add garlic, salt, cumin and coriander; cook and stir 1 minute. Stir in beans. Remove from heat.

2. Pour 1 cup salsa in bottom of **CROCK-POT**® slow cooker. Arrange 3 tortillas in single layer, cutting the tortillas in half as needed to make them fit. Place 2 cups vegetable mixture over tortillas; sprinkle with ½ cup cheese. Repeat layering two more times. Layer with remaining 3 tortillas; top with 2 cups salsa. Sprinkle with remaining 1 cup cheese. Reserve remaining filling for another use.

3. Cover; cook on HIGH 2 hours or until cheese is bubbly and edges are lightly browned. Sprinkle with cilantro. Turn off heat. Let stand, uncovered, 10 minutes before serving.

MAKES 6 SERVINGS

SWEET POTATO AND BLACK BEAN CHIPOTLE CHILI

1 tablespoon vegetable oil

2 large onions, diced

3 tablespoons chili powder

2 tablespoons tomato paste

1 tablespoon chipotle chili powder

1 tablespoon minced garlic

2 teaspoons salt

1 teaspoon ground cumin

1 cup water

2 large sweet potatoes, peeled and cut into ½-inch pieces (about 2 pounds)

2 cans (about 15 ounces *each*) black beans, rinsed and drained

2 cans (28 ounces *each*) crushed tomatoes

Optional toppings: sliced green onions, shredded Cheddar cheese and/or tortilla chips

1. Heat oil in large skillet over medium-high heat. Add onions; cook 8 minutes or until lightly browned and softened. Add chili powder, tomato paste, chipotle chili powder, garlic, salt and cumin; cook and stir 1 minute. Add water, scraping up any brown bits from bottom of skillet. Remove to **CROCK-POT®** slow cooker. Add potatoes, beans and tomatoes.

2. Cover; cook on LOW 8 hours or on HIGH 4 hours. Ladle into individual bowls. Top with desired toppings.

MAKES 8 TO 10 SERVINGS

KOSHARI

6 cups water

1 cup uncooked white basmati rice, rinsed and drained

1 cup dried brown lentils, rinsed and sorted

3 teaspoons kosher salt, divided

1 teaspoon ground cinnamon, divided

½ teaspoon ground nutmeg, divided

1 cup uncooked elbow macaroni

4 tablespoons olive oil, divided

1 large onion, thinly sliced

1 large onion, diced

1 tablespoon minced garlic

1 teaspoon ground cumin

½ teaspoon ground coriander

¼ teaspoon red pepper flakes

¼ teaspoon black pepper

1 can (28 ounces) crushed tomatoes

2 teaspoons red wine vinegar

1. Place water, rice, lentils, 2 teaspoons salt, ½ teaspoon cinnamon and ¼ teaspoon nutmeg in **CROCK-POT**® slow cooker. Cover; cook on HIGH 2 to 3 hours. Stir in macaroni. Cover; cook on HIGH 30 minutes, stirring halfway through cooking time.

2. Meanwhile, heat 2 tablespoons oil in large skillet over medium-high heat. Add sliced onion; cook 12 minutes or until edges are dark brown and onion is softened. Remove onion to medium bowl, using slotted spoon. Season with ¼ teaspoon salt. Set aside.

3. Heat same skillet with 2 tablespoons oil over medium heat. Add diced onion; cook 8 minutes or until softened. Add garlic, cumin, coriander, remaining ½ teaspoon cinnamon, red pepper flakes, black pepper and remaining ¼ teaspoon nutmeg; cook 30 seconds or until fragrant. Stir in tomatoes and remaining ¾ teaspoon salt; cook 8 to 10 minutes or until thickened, stirring occasionally. Stir in vinegar.

4. Fluff rice mixture lightly before scooping into individual bowls. Top each serving evenly with tomato sauce and reserved onions.

MAKES 6 TO 8 SERVINGS

HEARTY VEGETARIAN MAC AND CHEESE

1 can (about 14 ounces) stewed tomatoes, undrained

1½ cups prepared Alfredo sauce

1½ cups (6 ounces) shredded mozzarella cheese, divided

8 ounces whole grain pasta (medium shells or penne shape), cooked and drained

7 ounces Italian-flavored vegetarian sausage links, ¼-inch slices

¾ cup fresh basil leaves, thinly sliced and divided

½ cup vegetable broth

½ teaspoon salt

2 tablespoons grated Parmesan cheese

1. Coat inside of **CROCK-POT**® slow cooker with nonstick cooking spray. Add tomatoes, Alfredo sauce, 1 cup mozzarella cheese, pasta, sausage, ½ cup basil, broth and salt to **CROCK-POT**® slow cooker; stir to blend. Top with remaining ½ cup mozzarella cheese and Parmesan cheese.

2. Cover; cook on LOW 3½ hours or on HIGH 2 hours. Top with remaining ¼ cup basil.

MAKES 6 SERVINGS

TOFU, BLACK BEAN AND CORN CHILI BURRITOS

1 can (about 15 ounces) black
    beans, rinsed and drained

1 can (about 14 ounces) diced
    tomatoes with green pepper,
    celery and onion

8 ounces firm tofu, crumbled

1 cup mild prepared salsa

1 cup vegetable broth

½ cup frozen corn

1 tablespoon chili powder

1 teaspoon ground cumin

½ teaspoon ground chipotle
    pepper

½ teaspoon dried oregano

2 cups cooked rice

8 (6-inch) flour tortillas

Optional toppings: sliced
    avocado, sour cream, lettuce
    and/or chopped fresh cilantro

1. Combine beans, tomatoes, tofu, salsa, broth, corn, chili powder, cumin,
    chipotle pepper and oregano in **CROCK-POT**® slow cooker; stir to blend.
    Cover; cook on LOW 8 hours or on HIGH 4 hours.

2. Stir rice into bean mixture. Cover; cook on HIGH 15 minutes. Top each
    tortilla with about 1¼ cups bean mixture. Fold short ends of each tortilla
    over part of filling then roll up jelly-roll style. Serve with desired toppings.

MAKES 8 SERVINGS

ARTICHOKE PASTA

1 tablespoon olive oil

1 cup chopped sweet onion

4 cloves garlic, minced

1 can (28 ounces) crushed tomatoes

1 can (about 14 ounces) artichoke hearts, drained and cut into pieces

1 cup small pimiento-stuffed olives

¾ teaspoon red pepper flakes

8 ounces hot cooked fettuccine pasta

½ cup grated Asiago or Romano cheese

Fresh basil leaves (optional)

1. Coat inside of **CROCK-POT**® slow cooker with nonstick cooking spray. Heat oil in small skillet over medium heat. Add onion; cook and stir 5 minutes. Add garlic; cook and stir 1 minute. Combine onion mixture, tomatoes, artichokes, olives and red pepper flakes in **CROCK-POT**® slow cooker; stir to blend.

2. Cover; cook on LOW 7 to 8 hours or on HIGH 3 to 4 hours. Top pasta with artichoke sauce and cheese. Garnish with basil.

MAKES 4 SERVINGS

BLACK BEAN MUSHROOM CHILI

1 tablespoon vegetable oil

2 cups (8 ounces) sliced baby bella or button mushrooms

1 cup chopped onion

4 cloves garlic, minced

1 can (about 15 ounces) black beans, rinsed and drained

1 can (about 14 ounces) fire-roasted diced tomatoes

1 cup salsa

1 yellow or green bell pepper, finely diced

2 teaspoons chili powder or ground cumin

Sour cream (optional)

1. Coat inside of **CROCK-POT**® slow cooker with nonstick cooking spray. Heat oil in large skillet over medium heat. Add mushrooms, onion and garlic; cook 8 minutes or until mushrooms have released their liquid and liquid has thickened slightly.

2. Combine mushroom mixture, beans, tomatoes, salsa, bell pepper and chili powder in **CROCK-POT**® slow cooker; stir to blend. Cover; cook on LOW 5 to 6 hours or on HIGH 2½ to 3 hours. Ladle into shallow bowls. Top with sour cream, if desired.

MAKES 4 SERVINGS

SHREDDED CHICKEN TACOS

2 pounds boneless, skinless chicken thighs

½ cup prepared mango salsa, plus additional for serving

Lettuce (optional)

8 (6-inch) yellow corn tortillas, warmed

1. Coat inside of **CROCK-POT**® slow cooker with nonstick cooking spray. Add chicken and ½ cup salsa. Cover; cook on LOW 4 to 5 hours or on HIGH 2½ to 3 hours.

2. Remove chicken to large cutting board; shred with two forks. Stir shredded chicken back into **CROCK-POT**® slow cooker. To serve, divide chicken and lettuce, if desired, evenly among tortillas. Serve with additional salsa.

MAKES 4 SERVINGS

SWEET AND SPICY PORK PICADILLO

1 tablespoon olive oil

1 yellow onion, cut into ¼-inch pieces

2 cloves garlic, minced

1 pound boneless pork country-style ribs, trimmed and cut into 1-inch cubes

1 can (about 14 ounces) diced tomatoes

3 tablespoons cider vinegar

2 canned chipotle peppers in adobo sauce, chopped*

½ cup raisins

½ teaspoon ground cumin

½ teaspoon ground cinnamon

Hot cooked rice (optional)

Black beans (optional)

*You may substitute dried chipotle peppers, soaked in warm water about 20 minutes to soften before chopping.

1. Heat oil in large skillet over medium-low heat. Add onion and garlic; cook and stir 4 minutes. Add pork; cook and stir 5 to 7 minutes or until browned. Remove to **CROCK-POT**® slow cooker.

2. Add tomatoes, vinegar, chipotle peppers, raisins, cumin and cinnamon to **CROCK-POT**® slow cooker; stir to blend. Cover; cook on LOW 5 hours or on HIGH 3 hours. Remove pork to large cutting board; shred with two forks. Return pork to **CROCK-POT**® slow cooker; stir to blend. Cover; cook on HIGH 30 minutes. Serve with rice and beans, if desired.

MAKES 4 SERVINGS

CHICKEN AND SPICY BLACK BEAN TACOS

1 can (about 15 ounces) black beans, rinsed and drained

1 can (10 ounces) diced tomatoes with mild green chiles, drained

1½ teaspoons chili powder

¾ teaspoon ground cumin

1 teaspoon extra virgin olive oil

12 ounces boneless, skinless chicken breasts

12 crisp corn taco shells

Optional toppings: shredded lettuce, diced tomatoes, shredded Cheddar cheese, sour cream and/or sliced black olives

1. Coat inside of **CROCK-POT** slow cooker with nonstick cooking spray. Add beans and tomatoes with chiles. Combine chili powder, cumin and oil in small bowl; rub onto chicken. Place chicken in **CROCK-POT** slow cooker. Cover; cook on HIGH 1 to 2 hours.

2. Remove chicken to large cutting board; cut into ½-inch slices. Remove bean mixture to large bowl using slotted spoon.

3. To serve, warm taco shells according to package directions. Fill with equal amounts of bean mixture and chicken. Top as desired.

MAKES 6 SERVINGS

ARROZ CON QUESO

1 can (about 14 ounces) crushed tomatoes, undrained

1 can (about 15 ounces) black beans, rinsed and drained

1½ cups uncooked converted long grain rice

1 onion, chopped

1 cup cottage cheese

1 can (4 ounces) chopped mild green chiles

2 tablespoons vegetable oil

3 teaspoons minced garlic

2 cups (8 ounces) shredded Monterey Jack cheese, divided

Sliced jalapeño pepper (optional)*

Jalapeño peppers can sting and irritate the skin, so wear rubber gloves when handling peppers and do not touch your eyes.

Combine tomatoes, beans, rice, onion, cottage cheese, chiles, oil, garlic and 1 cup cheese in **CROCK-POT**® slow cooker; stir to blend. Cover; cook on LOW 6 to 9 hours or until liquid is absorbed. Sprinkle with remaining 1 cup cheese before serving. Garnish with jalapeño pepper.

MAKES 8 TO 10 SERVINGS

MEXICAN CARNITAS

1 boneless pork shoulder roast
    (2 pounds)

1 tablespoon garlic salt

1 tablespoon black pepper

1½ teaspoons adobo seasoning

1 medium onion, chopped

1 can (16 ounces) green salsa

½ cup water

¼ cup chopped fresh cilantro

Juice of 2 medium limes

3 cloves garlic, minced

4 (6-inch) flour tortillas, warmed

Optional toppings: chopped
    green bell pepper, tomatoes
    and red onion

Lime wedges (optional)

1. Coat inside of **CROCK-POT®** slow cooker with nonstick cooking spray.
   Season pork with garlic salt, black pepper and adobo seasoning.

2. Place pork, onion, salsa, water, cilantro, lime juice and garlic in **CROCK-POT®**
   slow cooker. Cover; cook on LOW 4 to 5 hours. Serve in tortillas with desired
   toppings. Garnish with lime wedges.

MAKES 4 SERVINGS

POBLANO CREAMED CORN

4 whole poblano peppers

3 tablespoons olive oil

1 package (16 ounces) frozen corn

3 slices American cheese

4 ounces cream cheese

2 tablespoons butter

1½ tablespoons chicken broth

1 tablespoon chopped jalapeño pepper (optional)*

Salt and black pepper

*Jalapeño peppers can sting and irritate the skin, so wear rubber gloves when handling peppers and do not touch your eyes.

1. Preheat oven to 350°F. Spray large baking sheet with nonstick cooking spray. Place poblano peppers on prepared baking sheet; brush with oil. Bake 20 minutes or until outer skins loosen. When cool enough to handle, remove outer skin from 1 poblano pepper and mince. Cut remaining 3 poblano peppers in half and reserve.

2. Combine corn, American cheese, minced poblano pepper, cream cheese, butter, broth, jalapeño pepper, if desired, salt and black pepper in **CROCK-POT®** slow cooker. Cover; cook on LOW 4 to 5 hours. To serve, spoon corn into reserved poblano pepper halves.

MAKES 6 SERVINGS

CONFETTI BLACK BEANS

1 cup dried black beans, rinsed and sorted

1½ teaspoons olive oil

1 medium onion, chopped

¼ cup chopped red bell pepper

¼ cup chopped yellow bell pepper

1 jalapeño pepper, finely chopped*

1 large tomato, chopped

½ teaspoon salt

⅛ teaspoon black pepper

2 cloves garlic, minced

1 can (about 14 ounces) chicken broth

1 whole bay leaf

Hot pepper sauce (optional)

*Jalapeño peppers can sting and irritate the skin, so wear rubber gloves when handling peppers and do not touch your eyes.

1. Place beans in large bowl and add enough cold water to cover by at least 2 inches. Soak 6 to 8 hours or overnight.** Drain beans; discard water.

2. Heat oil in large skillet over medium heat. Add onion, bell peppers and jalapeño pepper; cook and stir 5 minutes or until onion is tender. Add tomato, salt and black pepper; cook 5 minutes. Stir in garlic.

3. Place beans, broth and bay leaf in **CROCK-POT**® slow cooker. Add onion mixture. Cover; cook on LOW 7 to 8 hours or on HIGH 4½ to 5 hours. Remove and discard bay leaf. Serve with hot pepper sauce, if desired.

*To quick soak beans, place beans in large saucepan; cover with water. Bring to a boil over high heat. Boil 2 minutes. Remove from heat; let soak, covered, 1 hour.

MAKES 6 SERVINGS

ANCHO CHILE AND LIME PORK TACOS

2 large plantain leaves

1 boneless pork shoulder roast or pork chops (4 to 6 pounds)*

Juice of 4 to 5 medium limes

1 package (about 1 ounce) ancho chile paste

Salt

1 large onion, sliced

Pickled Red Onions (recipe follows)

Flour tortillas

Optional toppings: salsa, sour cream, guacamole, shredded cheese, lime slices and/or hot pepper sauce

*Unless you have a 5-, 6- or 7-quart **CROCK-POT**® slow cooker, cut any roast larger than 2½ pounds in half so it cooks completely.

1. Line **CROCK-POT**® slow cooker with plantain leaves; top with pork roast. Combine lime juice, chile paste and salt in medium bowl; stir until well blended. Add paste mixture and onion to **CROCK-POT**® slow cooker; wrap leaves over pork. Cover; cook on LOW 8 to 10 hours.

2. Meanwhile, prepare Pickled Red Onions.

3. Serve with Pickled Red Onions and tortillas; top as desired.

MAKES 10 TO 12 SERVINGS

PICKLED RED ONIONS: Combine 1 cup sliced red onion and juice from 1 to 2 limes in small bowl; set aside until juice is absorbed. Makes 1 cup.

FRIJOLES BORRACHOS

6 slices bacon, chopped

1 medium yellow onion, chopped

1 tablespoon minced garlic

3 jalapeño peppers, seeded and finely diced*

1 tablespoon dried oregano

1 can (12 ounces) beer

6 cups water

1 pound dried pinto beans, rinsed and sorted

1 can (about 14 ounces) diced tomatoes

1 tablespoon salt

¼ cup chopped fresh cilantro

*Jalapeño peppers can sting and irritate the skin, so wear rubber gloves when handling peppers and do not touch your eyes.

1. Heat large skillet over medium-high heat. Add bacon; cook 5 minutes or until mostly browned and crisp. Remove to **CROCK-POT**® slow cooker. Discard all but 3 tablespoons of drippings.

2. Heat same skillet over medium heat. Add onion; cook 6 minutes or until softened and lightly browned. Add garlic, jalapeño peppers and oregano; cook 30 seconds or until fragrant. *Increase heat to medium-high.* Add beer; bring to a simmer. Cook 2 minutes, stirring to scrape up any brown bits from bottom of skillet. Remove mixture to **CROCK-POT**® slow cooker.

3. Add water, beans, tomatoes and salt to **CROCK-POT**® slow cooker. Cover; cook on LOW 7 hours or on HIGH 3 to 4 hours. Mash beans slightly until broth is thickened and creamy. Top with cilantro.

MAKES 8 SERVINGS

TURKEY TACOS

1 pound ground turkey

1 medium onion, chopped

1 can (6 ounces) tomato paste

½ cup chunky salsa

1 tablespoon chopped fresh
   cilantro

½ teaspoon salt

1 tablespoon butter

1 tablespoon all-purpose flour

¼ teaspoon salt

⅓ cup milk

½ cup sour cream

   Pinch ground red pepper

8 taco shells

1. Brown turkey and onion in large skillet over medium heat, stirring to break up meat. Combine turkey mixture, tomato paste, salsa, cilantro and salt in **CROCK-POT**® slow cooker. Cover; cook on LOW 4 to 5 hours.

2. Just before serving, melt butter in small saucepan over low heat. Whisk in flour and salt; cook 1 minute. Whisk in milk; cook and stir over low heat until thickened. Remove from heat. Combine sour cream and ground red pepper in small bowl. Stir into hot milk mixture. Cook over low heat 1 minute, stirring constantly.

3. Spoon ¼ cup turkey mixture into each taco shell; top with sauce.

MAKES 8 SERVINGS

RED BEANS AND RICE

2 cans (about 15 ounces *each*) red beans, undrained

1 can (about 14 ounces) diced tomatoes

½ cup chopped celery

½ cup chopped green bell pepper

½ cup chopped green onions

2 cloves garlic, minced

1 to 2 teaspoons hot pepper sauce

1 teaspoon Worcestershire sauce

1 whole bay leaf

3 cups hot cooked rice

1. Combine beans, tomatoes, celery, bell pepper, green onions, garlic, hot pepper sauce, Worcestershire sauce and bay leaf in **CROCK-POT**® slow cooker; stir to blend. Cover; cook on LOW 4 to 6 hours or on HIGH 2 to 3 hours.

2. Mash bean mixture slightly in **CROCK-POT**® slow cooker until mixture thickens. Cover; cook on HIGH ½ to 1 hour. Remove and discard bay leaf. Serve bean mixture over rice.

MAKES 6 SERVINGS

SPICY SHREDDED BEEF TACOS

1 boneless beef chuck roast
  (2½ pounds)

1¼ teaspoons salt, divided

1 teaspoon *each* ground cumin,
  garlic powder and smoked
  paprika

2 tablespoons olive oil, divided

2 cups beef broth

1 red bell pepper, sliced

1 tomato, cut into wedges

½ onion, sliced

2 cloves garlic, minced

1 to 2 canned chipotle peppers
  in adobo sauce

Juice of 1 lime

Corn or flour tortillas, warmed

Optional toppings: sliced bell
  peppers, avocado, diced
  onion, lime wedges and/or
  chopped fresh cilantro

1. Season beef with 1 teaspoon salt, cumin, garlic powder and smoked
   paprika. Heat 1 tablespoon oil in large skillet over medium-high heat. Add
   beef; cook 5 minutes on each side until browned. Remove to **CROCK-POT**®
   slow cooker.

2. Pour in broth. Cover; cook on LOW 8 to 9 hours or on HIGH 4 to 5 hours.

3. Meanwhile, preheat oven to 425°F. Combine bell pepper, tomato, onion
   and garlic on large baking sheet. Drizzle with remaining 1 tablespoon oil.
   Roast 40 minutes or until vegetables are tender. Place vegetables, chipotle
   pepper, lime juice and remaining ¼ teaspoon salt in food processor or
   blender; blend until smooth.

4. Remove beef to large cutting board; shred with two forks. Combine
   shredded meat with 1 cup cooking liquid. Discard remaining cooking liquid.
   Serve on tortillas with sauce. Top as desired.

MAKES 6 TO 8 SERVINGS

SLOW-COOKED SHAKSHUKA

¼ cup extra virgin olive oil

1 medium onion, chopped

1 large red bell pepper, chopped

3 cloves garlic, sliced

1 can (28 ounces) crushed tomatoes with basil, garlic and oregano

2 teaspoons paprika

2 teaspoons ground cumin

2 teaspoons sugar

½ teaspoon salt

¼ teaspoon red pepper flakes

¾ cup crumbled feta cheese

6 eggs

Chopped fresh cilantro (optional)

Black pepper (optional)

Toasted baguette slices (optional)

1. Coat inside of **CROCK-POT**® slow cooker with nonstick cooking spray. Combine oil, onion, bell pepper, garlic, tomatoes, paprika, cumin, sugar, salt and red pepper flakes in **CROCK-POT**® slow cooker; stir to blend. Cover; cook on HIGH 3 hours. Stir in feta cheese. Break eggs, one at a time, onto top of tomato mixture, leaving a little space between each.

2. Cover; cook on HIGH 15 to 18 minutes or until egg whites are set but yolks are still creamy. Scoop eggs and sauce evenly into each serving dish. Garnish with cilantro and black pepper. Serve with baguette slices, if desired.

MAKES 6 SERVINGS

CHICKEN AND WILD RICE CASSEROLE

3 tablespoons olive oil

2 slices bacon, chopped

1½ pounds chicken thighs, trimmed

½ cup diced onion

½ cup diced celery

2 tablespoons Worcestershire sauce

½ teaspoon salt

¼ teaspoon black pepper

½ teaspoon dried sage

1 cup uncooked converted long grain white rice

1 package (4 ounces) wild rice

6 ounces brown mushrooms, wiped clean and quartered*

3 cups hot chicken broth**

2 tablespoons chopped fresh Italian parsley (optional)

You may substitute white button mushrooms, baby bellas or cremini mushrooms.

Use enough broth to cover chicken.

1. Spread oil on bottom of **CROCK-POT**® slow cooker. Microwave bacon on HIGH 1 minute. Remove to **CROCK-POT**® slow cooker. Place chicken in **CROCK-POT**® slow cooker, skin side down. Add onion, celery, Worcestershire sauce, salt, pepper, sage, white rice, wild rice, mushrooms and broth.

2. Cover; cook on LOW 3 to 4 hours or until rice is tender. Turn off heat. Uncover; let stand 15 minutes before serving. Remove chicken skin, if desired. Garnish with chopped parsley.

MAKES 4 TO 6 SERVINGS

CHICKEN SCALOPPINE IN ALFREDO SAUCE

2 tablespoons all-purpose flour

¼ teaspoon salt

¼ teaspoon black pepper

6 boneless, skinless chicken tenderloins (about 1 pound), cut lengthwise in half

1 tablespoon butter

1 tablespoon olive oil

1 cup Alfredo pasta sauce

1 package (12 ounces) uncooked spinach noodles

1. Place flour, salt and pepper in large bowl; stir to combine. Add chicken; toss to coat. Heat butter and oil in large skillet over medium-high heat. Add chicken; cook 3 minutes per side or until browned. Remove chicken to **CROCK-POT**® slow cooker.

2. Add pasta sauce to **CROCK-POT**® slow cooker. Cover; cook on LOW 1 to 1½ hours.

3. Meanwhile, cook noodles according to package directions. Drain; place in large shallow bowl. Spoon chicken and sauce over noodles.

MAKES 6 SERVINGS

VEGETABLE-STUFFED PORK CHOPS

4 bone-in pork chops
   Salt and black pepper
1 cup frozen corn
1 medium green bell pepper, chopped
½ cup Italian-style seasoned dry bread crumbs

1 small onion, chopped
½ cup uncooked converted long grain rice
1 can (8 ounces) tomato sauce

1. Cut pocket into each pork chop, cutting from edge to bone. Lightly season pockets with salt and black pepper. Combine corn, bell pepper, bread crumbs, onion and rice in large bowl; stir to blend. Stuff pork chops with rice mixture. Secure open side with toothpicks.

2. Place any remaining rice mixture in **CROCK-POT**® slow cooker. Add stuffed pork chops to **CROCK-POT**® slow cooker. Pour tomato sauce over pork chops. Cover; cook on LOW 8 to 10 hours.

3. Remove pork chops to large serving platter. Remove and discard toothpicks. Serve with extra rice mixture.

MAKES 4 SERVINGS

PIZZA-STYLE MOSTACCIOLI

1 jar (24 to 26 ounces) marinara sauce or tomato-basil pasta sauce

½ cup water

2 cups (6 ounces) uncooked mostaccioli pasta

1 package (8 ounces) sliced mushrooms

1 small yellow or green bell pepper, finely diced

½ cup (1 ounce) sliced pepperoni, halved

1 teaspoon dried oregano

¼ teaspoon red pepper flakes

1 cup (4 ounces) shredded pizza cheese blend or Italian cheese blend

Chopped fresh oregano (optional)

Garlic bread (optional)

1. Coat inside of **CROCK-POT**® slow cooker with nonstick cooking spray. Combine marinara sauce and water in **CROCK-POT**® slow cooker. Stir in pasta, mushrooms, bell pepper, pepperoni, dried oregano and red pepper flakes; mix well. Cover; cook on LOW 2 hours or on HIGH 1 hour.

2. Stir well. Cover; cook on HIGH 45 minutes to 1 hour or until pasta and vegetables are tender. Spoon into shallow bowls. Top with cheese and garnish with fresh oregano. Serve with bread, if desired.

MAKES 4 SERVINGS

CHIPOTLE CHICKEN CASSEROLE

1 pound boneless, skinless chicken thighs, cut into cubes

1½ cups chicken broth

1 can (about 15 ounces) navy beans, rinsed and drained

1 can (about 15 ounces) black beans, rinsed and drained

1 can (about 14 ounces) crushed tomatoes, undrained

½ cup orange juice

1 medium onion, diced

1 canned chipotle pepper in adobo sauce, minced

1 teaspoon salt

1 teaspoon ground cumin

1 whole bay leaf

Combine chicken, broth, beans, tomatoes, orange juice, onion, chipotle pepper, salt, cumin and bay leaf in **CROCK-POT**® slow cooker; stir to blend. Cover; cook on LOW 7 to 8 hours or on HIGH 3½ to 4 hours. Remove and discard bay leaf before serving.

MAKES 6 SERVINGS

RAVIOLI CASSEROLE

8 ounces pork or turkey Italian sausage, casings removed

½ cup minced onion

1½ cups marinara sauce

1 can (about 14 ounces) Italian-style diced tomatoes

2 packages (9 ounces *each*) refrigerated meatless ravioli, such as wild mushroom or three cheese, divided

1½ cups (6 ounces) shredded mozzarella cheese, divided

Chopped fresh Italian parsley (optional)

1. Heat large skillet over medium-high heat. Brown sausage and onion 6 to 8 minutes, stirring to break up meat. Drain fat. Stir in marinara sauce and tomatoes; mix well. Remove from heat.

2. Coat inside of **CROCK-POT®** slow cooker with nonstick cooking spray. Spoon 1 cup sauce into **CROCK-POT®** slow cooker. Layer half of 1 package of ravioli over sauce; top with additional ½ cup sauce and ½ cup cheese. Repeat layers of ravioli and sauce; top with ½ cup cheese. Repeat layering with remaining package ravioli and all remaining sauce. Cover; cook on LOW 2½ to 3 hours or on HIGH 1½ to 2 hours or until sauce is heated through and ravioli is tender.

3. Sprinkle remaining ½ cup cheese over top of casserole. Cover; cook on HIGH 15 minutes or until cheese is melted. Garnish with parsley.

MAKES 4 TO 6 SERVINGS

COQ AU VIN WITH LIMA BEANS

4 pounds chicken thighs and drumsticks

3 slices bacon, cut into pieces

4 cups chicken broth

1 cup sliced mushrooms

1 cup sliced carrots

1 cup dry red wine

½ cup pearl onions

⅓ cup whiskey

3 to 4 cloves garlic, chopped

2 tablespoons tomato paste

1½ teaspoons herbes de Provence

2 whole bay leaves

Salt and black pepper

1 tablespoon water

2 tablespoons all-purpose flour

1 cup lima beans

Chopped fresh Italian parsley (optional)

Roasted red potatoes, quartered (optional)

1. Coat inside of **CROCK-POT®** slow cooker with nonstick cooking spray. Add chicken and bacon to **CROCK-POT®** slow cooker. Cover; cook on HIGH 45 minutes, turning chicken halfway through cooking time.

2. Turn **CROCK-POT®** slow cooker to LOW. Stir in broth, mushrooms, carrots, wine, onions, whiskey, garlic, tomato paste, herbes de Provence, bay leaves, salt and pepper. Stir water into flour in small bowl until smooth; whisk into **CROCK-POT®** slow cooker.

3. Cover; cook on LOW 6 hours. Add beans to **CROCK-POT®** slow cooker during last 10 minutes of cooking. Remove and discard bay leaves. Garnish with parsley. Serve with potatoes, if desired.

MAKES 8 TO 10 SERVINGS

CHEESEBURGER POTATO CASSEROLE

1 pound ground beef

½ cup chopped onion

1 can (about 10¾ ounces) Cheddar cheese soup

¼ cup sweet pickle relish

2 tablespoons brown mustard

2 tablespoons ketchup, plus additional for topping

1 tablespoon Worcestershire sauce

1 package (30 ounces) shredded potatoes

2 cups (8 ounces) shredded Cheddar cheese

1 teaspoon salt

½ teaspoon black pepper

Green onions (optional)

1. Coat inside of **CROCK-POT**® slow cooker with nonstick cooking spray. Brown beef and onion in large skillet over medium-high heat 6 to 8 minutes, stirring to break up meat. Drain fat. Stir in cheese soup, relish, mustard, 2 tablespoons ketchup and Worcestershire sauce until well blended.

2. Arrange half of potatoes in bottom of **CROCK-POT**® slow cooker. Spoon half of meat mixture over potatoes. Sprinkle with 1½ cups cheese, ½ teaspoon salt and ¼ teaspoon pepper. Top with remaining half of potatoes. Add remaining half of meat mixture; sprinkle with remaining ½ cup cheese, ½ teaspoon salt and ¼ teaspoon pepper.

3. Cover; cook on LOW 4 hours or on HIGH 2 hours. Top with additional ketchup and green onions, if desired.

MAKES 6 SERVINGS

PASTA SHELLS WITH PROSCIUTTO

3 cups (8 ounces) uncooked
medium shell pasta

1 jar (24 to 26 ounces) vodka
pasta sauce

¾ cup water

½ cup whipping cream

2 ounces (½ cup) torn or coarsely
chopped thin sliced prosciutto

¼ cup chopped fresh chives

1. Coat inside of **CROCK-POT**® slow cooker with nonstick cooking spray.
   Combine pasta, pasta sauce and water in **CROCK-POT**® slow cooker; stir
   to blend. Cover; cook on LOW 2 hours or on HIGH 1 hour.

2. Stir in cream. Cover; cook on LOW 1 to 1½ hours or on HIGH 45 minutes to
   1 hour or until pasta is tender.

3. Stir prosciutto into pasta mixture. Spoon into shallow bowls; top with
   chives.

MAKES 4 SERVINGS

HAM AND POTATO CASSEROLE

1½ pounds red potatoes, unpeeled and sliced

8 ounces thinly sliced extra-lean deli ham

2 poblano chile peppers, cut into thin slices

2 tablespoons olive oil

2 teaspoons dried oregano

¼ teaspoon salt

1 cup (4 ounces) shredded Monterey Jack cheese

2 tablespoons finely chopped fresh cilantro

1. Combine potatoes, ham, chile peppers, oil, oregano and salt in **CROCK-POT**® slow cooker; stir to blend. Cover; cook on LOW 7 hours or on HIGH 4 hours.

2. Remove potato mixture to large serving platter. Sprinkle with cheese and cilantro; let stand 3 minutes or until cheese is melted.

MAKES 6 SERVINGS

SIMPLY DELICIOUS PORK ROAST

1½ pounds boneless pork loin, cut into 6 pieces *or* 6 boneless pork loin chops

4 medium Golden Delicious apples, cored and sliced

3 tablespoons packed light brown sugar

1 teaspoon ground cinnamon

½ teaspoon salt

1. Place pork in **CROCK-POT**® slow cooker; cover with apples.

2. Combine brown sugar, cinnamon and salt in small bowl; sprinkle over apples. Cover; cook on LOW 6 to 8 hours.

MAKES 6 SERVINGS

COUNTRY CHICKEN AND VEGETABLES WITH CREAMY HERB SAUCE

1 pound new potatoes, cut into ½-inch wedges

1 medium onion, cut into 8 wedges

½ cup coarsely chopped celery

4 bone-in chicken drumsticks, skinned

4 bone-in chicken thighs, skinned

1 can (10¾ ounces) cream of chicken soup

1 package (1 ounce) ranch-style dressing mix

½ teaspoon dried thyme

¼ teaspoon black pepper

½ cup whipping cream

Salt

¼ cup finely chopped green onions (green and white parts) (optional)

1. Coat inside of **CROCK-POT**® slow cooker with nonstick cooking spray. Arrange potatoes, onion and celery in bottom. Add chicken. Combine soup, dressing mix, thyme and pepper in small bowl; stir to blend. Spoon mixture evenly over chicken and vegetables.

2. Cover; cook on HIGH 3½ hours. Transfer chicken to shallow serving bowl with slotted spoon. Add cream and salt, if desired, to cooking liquid. Stir well to blend. Pour sauce over chicken. Garnish with green onions.

MAKES 4 SERVINGS

TWICE "BAKED" POTATOES

4 baking potatoes
   (about 10 ounces *each*)

3 tablespoons olive oil, divided

1 head garlic

¼ cup sour cream

1 to 2 tablespoons milk

½ teaspoon salt

¼ teaspoon black pepper

2 slices bacon, cooked and
   crumbled

½ cup (2 ounces) shredded
   Cheddar cheese, divided

¼ teaspoon smoked paprika

Chopped green onions
   (optional)

1. Rub potatoes with 2 tablespoons oil; wrap each potato in foil. Place potatoes in **CROCK-POT®** slow cooker. Cut across top of garlic head. Place garlic in foil; top with remaining 1 tablespoon oil. Twist foil closed around garlic; place on top of potatoes. Cover; cook on HIGH 4 hours or until potatoes are soft when pierced with knife.

2. Pull foil away from each potato; crimp it around bottom of potatoes. Cut thin slice from top of each potato. Scoop inside of potatoes into large bowl, leaving about ¼-inch shell. Squeeze garlic head to remove softened cloves; mash with fork. Measure 1 tablespoon mashed garlic; add to large bowl with potatoes. Refrigerate any remaining garlic in airtight jar for another use.

3. Add sour cream, milk, salt and pepper to large bowl with potatoes; beat with electric mixer at medium speed 3 to 4 minutes or until smooth. Stir in bacon and half of cheese. Spoon mashed potatoes into shells, mounding at top. Top with remaining cheese and paprika. Return potatoes to **CROCK-POT®** slow cooker. Cover; cook on HIGH 15 minutes or until cheese is melted. Garnish with green onions.

MAKES 4 SERVINGS

PARMESAN POTATO WEDGES

2 pounds red potatoes, cut into ½-inch wedges

¼ cup finely chopped yellow onion

1½ teaspoons dried oregano

½ teaspoon salt

¼ teaspoon black pepper

2 tablespoons butter, cubed

¼ cup grated Parmesan cheese

Layer potatoes, onion, oregano, salt and pepper in **CROCK-POT**® slow cooker; dot with butter. Cover; cook on HIGH 4 hours. Remove potatoes to large serving platter; sprinkle with cheese.

MAKES 6 SERVINGS

GRATIN POTATOES WITH ASIAGO CHEESE

6 slices bacon, cut into 1-inch pieces

6 medium baking potatoes, peeled and thinly sliced

½ cup grated Asiago cheese

Salt and black pepper

1½ cups whipping cream

1. Heat large skillet over medium heat. Add bacon; cook and stir until crisp. Remove to paper towel-lined plate using slotted spoon.

2. Pour bacon drippings into **CROCK-POT®** slow cooker. Layer one fourth of potatoes on bottom of **CROCK-POT®** slow cooker. Sprinkle one fourth of bacon over potatoes and top with one fourth of cheese. Season with salt and pepper.

3. Repeat layers three times. Pour cream over all. Cover; cook on LOW 7 to 9 hours or on HIGH 5 to 6 hours.

MAKES 4 TO 6 SERVINGS

BLUE CHEESE POTATOES

2 pounds red potatoes, peeled and cut into ½-inch pieces

1¼ cups chopped green onions, divided

2 tablespoons olive oil, divided

1 teaspoon dried basil

½ teaspoon salt

¼ teaspoon black pepper

½ cup crumbled blue cheese

1. Layer potatoes, 1 cup green onions, 1 tablespoon oil, basil, salt and pepper in **CROCK-POT®** slow cooker. Cover; cook on LOW 7 hours or on HIGH 4 hours.

2. Top with cheese and remaining 1 tablespoon oil. Cover; cook on HIGH 5 minutes. Remove potatoes to large serving bowl. Top with remaining ¼ cup green onions.

MAKES 5 SERVINGS

RUSTIC GARLIC MASHED POTATOES

2 pounds baking potatoes, unpeeled and cut into ½-inch cubes

¼ cup water

2 tablespoons unsalted butter, cubed

1¼ teaspoons salt

½ teaspoon garlic powder

¼ teaspoon black pepper

1 cup milk

Place potatoes, water, butter, salt, garlic powder and pepper in **CROCK-POT**® slow cooker; toss to blend. Cover; cook on LOW 7 hours or on HIGH 4 hours. Add milk to potatoes. Mash potatoes with potato masher until smooth.

MAKES 5 SERVINGS

LEMON-MINT RED POTATOES

2 pounds new red potatoes

3 tablespoons extra virgin olive oil

1 teaspoon salt

½ teaspoon Greek seasoning or
   dried oregano

¼ teaspoon garlic powder

¼ teaspoon black pepper

4 tablespoons chopped fresh mint,
   divided

2 tablespoons butter

2 tablespoons lemon juice

1 teaspoon grated lemon peel

1. Coat inside of **CROCK-POT®** slow cooker with nonstick cooking spray.
   Add potatoes and oil, stirring gently to coat. Sprinkle with salt, Greek
   seasoning, garlic powder and pepper.

2. Cover; cook on LOW 7 hours or on HIGH 4 hours. Stir in 2 tablespoons
   mint, butter, lemon juice and lemon peel until butter is completely melted.
   Cover; cook on HIGH 15 minutes. Sprinkle with remaining 2 tablespoons
   mint.

MAKES 4 SERVINGS

COCONUT-LIME SWEET POTATOES WITH WALNUTS

2½ pounds sweet potatoes, cut into 1-inch pieces

8 ounces shredded carrots

¾ cup shredded coconut, toasted and divided*

¼ cup (½ stick) butter, melted

3 tablespoons sugar

½ teaspoon salt

¾ cup walnuts, toasted, coarsely chopped and divided**

2 teaspoons grated lime peel

To toast coconut, spread in a single layer in heavy-bottomed skillet. Cook and stir 1 to 2 minutes or until lightly browned. Remove from skillet immediately.

**To toast walnuts, spread in single layer in small heavy skillet. Cook and stir over medium heat 1 to 2 minutes or until lightly browned.*

1. Combine potatoes, carrots, ½ cup coconut, butter, sugar and salt in **CROCK-POT**® slow cooker. Cover; cook on LOW 5 to 6 hours. Remove to large bowl.

2. Mash potatoes with potato masher. Stir in 3 tablespoons walnuts and lime peel. Sprinkle with remaining walnuts and toasted coconut.

MAKES 6 TO 8 SERVINGS

RUSTIC POTATOES AU GRATIN

½ cup milk

1 can (10¾ ounces) condensed Cheddar cheese soup, undiluted

1 package (8 ounces) cream cheese, softened

1 clove garlic, minced

¼ teaspoon ground nutmeg

⅛ teaspoon black pepper

2 pounds baking potatoes, unpeeled and cut into ¼-inch-thick slices

1 small onion, thinly sliced

Paprika (optional)

1. Heat milk in small saucepan over medium heat until small bubbles form around edge of pan. Remove from heat. Stir in soup, cream cheese, garlic, nutmeg and pepper until smooth.

2. Layer one fourth of potatoes and one fourth of onion in **CROCK-POT**® slow cooker. Top with one fourth of soup mixture. Repeat layers three times, using remaining potatoes, onion and soup mixture. Cover; cook on LOW 6 to 7 hours until most liquid is absorbed. Garnish with paprika.

MAKES 6 SERVINGS

CHUNKY RANCH POTATOES

3 pounds unpeeled red potatoes, quartered

1 cup water

½ cup ranch dressing

½ cup grated Parmesan or Cheddar cheese

¼ cup minced fresh chives

1. Place potatoes in **CROCK-POT**® slow cooker. Add water. Cover; cook on LOW 7 to 9 hours or on HIGH 4 to 6 hours.

2. Stir in ranch dressing, cheese and chives. Break up potatoes into large pieces.

MAKES 8 SERVINGS

MASHED RUTABAGAS AND POTATOES

2 pounds rutabagas, peeled and cut into ½-inch pieces

1 pound potatoes, peeled and cut into ½-inch pieces

½ cup milk

½ teaspoon ground nutmeg

2 tablespoons chopped fresh Italian parsley

Sprigs fresh Italian parsley (optional)

1. Place rutabagas and potatoes in **CROCK-POT**® slow cooker; add enough water to cover vegetables. Cover; cook on LOW 6 hours or on HIGH 3 hours. Remove vegetables to large bowl using slotted spoon. Discard cooking liquid.

2. Mash vegetables with potato masher. Add milk, nutmeg and chopped parsley; stir until smooth. Garnish with parsley sprigs.

MAKES 8 SERVINGS

CANDIED SWEET POTATOES

3 medium sweet potatoes (1½ to 2 pounds), sliced into ½-inch rounds

½ cup water

¼ cup (½ stick) butter, cut into small pieces

3 tablespoons sugar

1 tablespoon vanilla

1 teaspoon ground nutmeg

Combine potatoes, water, butter, sugar, vanilla and nutmeg in **CROCK-POT®** slow cooker; stir to blend. Cover; cook on LOW 7 hours or on HIGH 4 hours.

MAKES 4 SERVINGS

COLCANNON

6 tablespoons butter, cut into small pieces

3 pounds russet potatoes, peeled and cut into 1-inch pieces

2 medium leeks (white and light green parts only), thinly sliced

½ cup water

2½ teaspoons kosher salt

¼ teaspoon black pepper

1 cup milk

½ small head (about 1 pound) savoy cabbage, cored and thinly sliced

4 slices bacon, crisp-cooked and crumbled

1. Sprinkle butter on bottom of **CROCK-POT®** slow cooker. Layer half of potatoes, leeks, remaining potatoes, water, salt and pepper. Cover; cook on HIGH 5 hours or until potatoes are tender, stirring halfway through cooking time.

2. Mash potatoes in **CROCK-POT®** slow cooker until smooth. Stir in milk and cabbage. Cover; cook on HIGH 30 to 40 minutes or until cabbage is crisp-tender. Stir bacon into potato mixture.

MAKES 8 SERVINGS

CURRIED CAULIFLOWER AND POTATOES

3 tablespoons vegetable oil

1 medium onion, chopped

1 tablespoon minced garlic

1 tablespoon curry powder

1½ teaspoons salt

1½ teaspoons grated fresh ginger

1 teaspoon ground turmeric

1 teaspoon yellow or brown mustard seeds

¼ teaspoon red pepper flakes

1 medium head cauliflower, cut into 1-inch pieces

2 pounds fingerling potatoes, unpeeled and halved

½ cup water

1. Heat oil in medium skillet over medium heat. Add onion; cook 8 minutes or until softened. Add garlic, curry powder, salt, ginger, turmeric, mustard seeds and red pepper flakes; cook and stir 1 minute. Remove onion mixture to **CROCK-POT**® slow cooker.

2. Stir in cauliflower, potatoes and water. Cover; cook on HIGH 4 hours.

MAKES 6 SERVINGS

SCALLOPS IN FRESH TOMATO AND HERB SAUCE

2 tablespoons vegetable oil

1 medium red onion, peeled and diced

1 clove garlic, minced

3½ cups fresh tomatoes, peeled*

1 can (12 ounces) tomato pureé

1 can (6 ounces) tomato paste

¼ cup dry red wine

2 tablespoons chopped fresh Italian parsley

1 tablespoon chopped fresh oregano

¼ teaspoon black pepper

1½ pounds fresh scallops, cleaned and drained

Hot cooked pasta or rice (optional)

To peel tomatoes, place one at a time in simmering water about 10 seconds. (Add 30 seconds if tomatoes are not fully ripened.) Immediately plunge into a bowl of cold water for another 10 seconds. Peel skin with a knife.

1. Heat oil in medium skillet over medium heat. Add onion and garlic; cook and stir 7 to 8 minutes or until onion is soft and translucent. Remove to **CROCK-POT**® slow cooker.

2. Add tomatoes, tomato purée, tomato paste, wine, parsley, oregano and pepper. Cover; cook on LOW 6 to 8 hours.

3. Turn **CROCK-POT**® slow cooker to HIGH. Add scallops. Cover; cook on HIGH 15 minutes or until scallops are cooked through. Serve over pasta, if desired.

MAKES 4 SERVINGS

SOUTHWESTERN SALMON PO' BOYS

1 red bell pepper, sliced

1 green bell pepper, sliced

1 onion, sliced

½ teaspoon Southwest chipotle seasoning

¼ teaspoon salt

¼ teaspoon black pepper

4 salmon fillets (about 6 ounces *each*), rinsed and patted dry

½ cup Italian dressing

¼ cup water

4 large French sandwich rolls, split *or* French bread cut into 6-inch pieces and split

Chipotle mayonnaise*

Fresh cilantro (optional)

If unavailable, combine ¼ cup mayonnaise with ½ teaspoon adobo sauce or substitute regular mayonnaise.

1. Coat inside of **CROCK-POT**® slow cooker with nonstick cooking spray. Arrange half of sliced bell peppers and onion in bottom.

2. Combine chipotle seasoning, salt and black pepper in small bowl; rub over both sides of salmon. Place salmon on top of vegetables in **CROCK-POT**® slow cooker. Pour Italian dressing over salmon and top with remaining bell peppers and onion. Add water. Cover; cook on HIGH 1½ hours.

3. Toast rolls, if desired. Spread tops with chipotle mayonnaise and garnish with cilantro. Spoon 1 to 2 tablespoons cooking liquid onto roll bottoms. Place 1 salmon fillet on each roll (remove skin first, if desired). Top with vegetable mixture.

MAKES 4 SERVINGS

CREAMY SEAFOOD DIP

1 package (8 ounces) shredded
    pepper jack cheese

1 can (6 ounces) lump crabmeat,
    drained

1 pound cooked shrimp, peeled,
    deveined and chopped

1 cup whipping cream, divided

1 round sourdough bread loaf
    (about 1 pound)

1. Place cheese in **CROCK-POT**® slow cooker. Add crabmeat, shrimp and
   ¾ cup cream; stir to blend. Cover; cook on HIGH 10 to 15 minutes or until
   cheese is melted.

2. Meanwhile, cut off top of bread and hollow out to create bowl. Cut extra
   bread into large pieces. Place bread bowl on serving plate. Place extra
   bread around bowl.

3. Check consistency of dip. Stir in up to ¼ cup additional cream, as needed.
   Pour into bread bowl.

MAKES 6 TO 8 SERVINGS

BRAISED SEA BASS WITH AROMATIC VEGETABLES

2 tablespoons butter or olive oil

2 bulbs fennel, thinly sliced

3 large carrots, julienned

3 large leeks, cleaned and thinly sliced

Salt and black pepper

6 sea bass fillets or other firm-fleshed white fish (2 to 3 pounds *total*)

1. Melt butter in large skillet over medium-high heat. Add fennel, carrots and leeks; cook and stir 6 to 8 minutes or until beginning to soften and lightly brown. Season with salt and pepper. Arrange half of vegetables in bottom of **CROCK-POT**® slow cooker.

2. Season sea bass with salt and pepper; place on top of vegetables in **CROCK-POT**® slow cooker. Top with remaining vegetables. Cover; cook on LOW 2 to 3 hours or on HIGH 1 to 1½ hours.

MAKES 6 SERVINGS

ASIAN LETTUCE WRAPS

2 teaspoons canola oil

1½ pounds boneless, skinless chicken breasts or pork shoulder, chopped into ¼-inch pieces

2 leeks, trimmed and chopped into ¼-inch pieces

1 cup shiitake mushrooms, stems removed and caps chopped into ¼-inch pieces

1 stalk celery, chopped into ¼-inch pieces

1 tablespoon oyster sauce

1 tablespoon soy sauce

1 teaspoon dark sesame oil

¼ teaspoon black pepper

2 tablespoons water

1 bag (8 ounces) coleslaw or broccoli slaw mix

½ red bell pepper, cut into thin strips

½ pound large raw shrimp, peeled, deveined and cut into ¼-inch pieces

3 tablespoons unsalted dry roasted peanuts, coarsely chopped

Hoisin sauce

12 crisp romaine lettuce leaves with white rib removed, patted dry

Fresh whole chives

1. Heat canola oil in large skillet over medium-high heat. Add chicken; cook 6 to 8 minutes or until browned on all sides. Remove to **CROCK-POT**® slow cooker. Add leeks, mushrooms, celery, oyster sauce, soy sauce, sesame oil, black pepper and water to **CROCK-POT**® slow cooker. Toss slaw and bell pepper in medium bowl; place in single layer on top of chicken.

2. Cover; cook on LOW 4 to 5 hours or on HIGH 2 to 2½ hours. Stir in shrimp during last 20 minutes of cooking. When shrimp are pink and opaque, remove mixture to large bowl. Add chopped peanuts; mix well.

3. To serve, spread about 1 teaspoon hoisin sauce on each lettuce leaf. Add 1 to 2 tablespoons meat mixture and tightly roll; secure by tying chives around rolled leaves.

MAKES 6 SERVINGS

SWEET AND SOUR SHRIMP

1 can (16 ounces) sliced peaches in syrup, undrained

½ cup chopped green onions

½ cup chopped red bell pepper

½ cup chopped green bell pepper

½ cup chopped celery

⅓ cup vegetable broth

¼ cup soy sauce

2 tablespoons rice wine vinegar

2 tablespoons dark sesame oil

1 teaspoon red pepper flakes

¼ cup water

2 tablespoons cornstarch

1 package (6 ounces) snow peas

1 pound cooked medium shrimp

1 cup cherry tomatoes, cut into halves

½ cup toasted walnut pieces*

Hot cooked rice

To toast walnuts, spread in single layer in heavy skillet. Cook and stir over medium heat 1 to 2 minutes or until nuts are lightly browned.

1. Place peaches with syrup, green onions, bell peppers, celery, broth, soy sauce, vinegar, oil and red pepper flakes in **CROCK-POT**® slow cooker. Cover; cook on LOW 3 to 4 hours or on HIGH 2 to 3 hours or until vegetables are tender.

2. Stir water into cornstarch in small bowl until smooth; whisk into vegetable mixture. Stir in snow peas. Cover; cook on HIGH 15 minutes or until thickened.

3. Add shrimp, tomatoes and walnuts to **CROCK-POT**® slow cooker. Cover; cook on HIGH 5 minutes or until shrimp are pink and opaque. Stir to blend shrimp mixture before serving over rice.

MAKES 4 TO 6 SERVINGS

CAPE COD STEW

2 pounds medium raw shrimp, peeled and deveined

2 pounds fresh cod or other white fish

3 lobsters (1½ to 2½ pounds *each*), uncooked

1 pound mussels or clams, scrubbed

2 cans (about 14 ounces *each*) chopped tomatoes

4 cups beef broth

½ cup chopped onion

½ cup chopped carrot

½ cup chopped fresh cilantro

2 tablespoons sea salt

2 teaspoons minced garlic

2 teaspoons lemon juice

4 whole bay leaves

1 teaspoon dried thyme

½ teaspoon saffron threads

1. Cut shrimp and fish into bite-size pieces and place in large bowl; refrigerate. Remove lobster tails and claws. Chop tail into 2-inch pieces and separate claws at joints. Place lobster and mussels in large bowl; refrigerate.

2. Combine tomatoes, broth, onion, carrot, cilantro, salt, garlic, lemon juice, bay leaves, thyme and saffron in **CROCK-POT**® slow cooker; stir to blend. Cover; cook on LOW 7 hours.

3. Add seafood. Turn **CROCK-POT**® slow cooker to HIGH. Cover; cook on HIGH 45 minutes to 1 hour or until seafood is just cooked through. Remove and discard bay leaves. Discard any mussels that do not open.

MAKES 8 SERVINGS

BACON-WRAPPED SCALLOPS

24 sea scallops, side muscle
removed

½ cup Belgian white ale

3 tablespoons chopped fresh
cilantro

2 tablespoons honey

¼ teaspoon chipotle chili powder

12 slices bacon, halved

1. Pour ½ inch of water in bottom of **CROCK-POT**® slow cooker. Combine scallops, ale, cilantro, honey and chipotle chili powder in medium bowl; toss to coat. Refrigerate 30 minutes.

2. Place 1 scallop on end of 1 bacon half. Roll up jelly-roll style and secure with toothpick. Remove to large baking sheet. Repeat with remaining bacon and scallops. Brush tops of scallops with ale mixture.

3. Heat large skillet over medium heat. Add wrapped scallops; cook 5 to 7 minutes or until bacon begins to brown. Remove to **CROCK-POT**® slow cooker. Cover; cook on LOW 1 hour.

MAKES 8 SERVINGS

SHRIMP AND OKRA GUMBO

1 tablespoon olive oil

8 ounces kielbasa or smoked sausage, halved lengthwise and cut into ¼-inch-thick half slices

1 green bell pepper, chopped

1 medium onion, chopped

3 stalks celery, cut into ¼-inch slices

6 green onions, chopped

4 cloves garlic, minced

1 cup chicken broth

1 can (about 14 ounces) diced tomatoes

1 teaspoon Cajun seasoning

½ teaspoon dried thyme

1 pound large raw shrimp, peeled and deveined (with tails on)

2 cups frozen cut okra, thawed

1. Coat inside of **CROCK-POT**® slow cooker with nonstick cooking spray. Heat oil in large skillet over medium-high heat. Add kielbasa; cook and stir 4 minutes or until browned. Remove to **CROCK-POT**® slow cooker using slotted spoon.

2. Return skillet to medium-high heat. Add bell pepper, chopped onion, celery, green onions and garlic; cook and stir 5 to 6 minutes or until vegetables are crisp-tender. Remove to **CROCK-POT**® slow cooker. Stir in broth, tomatoes, Cajun seasoning and thyme.

3. Cover; cook on LOW 4 hours. Stir in shrimp and okra. Cover; cook on LOW 30 to 35 minutes.

MAKES 6 SERVINGS

CAJUN PORK SAUSAGE AND SHRIMP STEW

1 can (28 ounces) diced tomatoes

1 package (16 ounces) frozen mixed vegetables (potatoes, carrots, celery and onions)

1 package (14 to 16 ounces) kielbasa or smoked sausage, cut diagonally into ¾-inch-thick slices

2 teaspoons Cajun seasoning

¾ pound large raw shrimp, peeled and deveined (with tails on)

2 cups (8 ounces) frozen sliced okra, thawed

Hot cooked rice or grits

1. Coat inside of **CROCK-POT**® slow cooker with nonstick cooking spray. Combine tomatoes, vegetables, sausage and Cajun seasoning in **CROCK-POT**® slow cooker; stir to blend. Cover; cook on LOW 5 to 6 hours or on HIGH 2 to 2½ hours.

2. Stir shrimp and okra into **CROCK-POT**® slow cooker. Cover; cook on HIGH 30 to 35 minutes or until shrimp are opaque. Serve over rice.

MAKES 6 SERVINGS

MISO-POACHED SALMON

1½ cups water

2 green onions, cut into 2-inch long pieces, plus additional for garnish

¼ cup yellow miso paste

¼ cup soy sauce

2 tablespoons sake

2 tablespoons mirin

1½ teaspoons grated fresh ginger

1 teaspoon minced garlic

6 salmon fillets (4 ounces *each*)

Hot cooked rice

1. Combine water, 2 green onions, miso paste, soy sauce, sake, mirin, ginger and garlic in **CROCK-POT**® slow cooker; stir to blend. Cover; cook on HIGH 30 minutes.

2. Turn **CROCK-POT**® slow cooker to LOW. Add salmon, skin side down. Cover; cook on LOW 30 to 60 minutes or until salmon turns opaque and flakes easily with fork. Serve over rice with cooking liquid as desired. Garnish with additional green onions.

MAKES 6 SERVINGS

SPAGHETTI SQUASH WITH SHRIMP AND VEGGIES

1 spaghetti squash (3 pounds)

4 cups fresh baby spinach

1 orange or red bell pepper,
    cut into 1-inch squares

½ cup julienned sun-dried
    tomatoes (not packed in oil)

3 tablespoons prepared pesto

2 tablespoons olive oil

1 teaspoon salt

½ pound peeled cooked medium
    shrimp (with tails on)

¼ cup grated Parmesan cheese
    (optional)

1. Pierce squash evenly 10 times with knife. Place squash in **CROCK-POT**®
   slow cooker; add 1 inch water. Cover; cook on HIGH 2½ hours. Remove
   squash to large cutting board; let stand until cool enough to handle.

2. Meanwhile, pour off all but 2 tablespoons of water from **CROCK-POT**®
   slow cooker. Add spinach, bell pepper, tomatoes, pesto, oil and salt; stir
   to blend. Cover; cook on HIGH 5 minutes.

3. Cut squash in half lengthwise. Remove and discard seeds and fibers.
   Scoop pulp into shreds; return to **CROCK-POT**® slow cooker. Toss well
   with spinach mixture; place shrimp on top. Cover; cook on HIGH 15 to
   20 minutes or until shrimp are pink and opaque. Top each serving with
   cheese, if desired.

MAKES 4 SERVINGS

SOUPER SATURDAY

CHICKEN ORZO SOUP

1 tablespoon vegetable oil

1 onion, diced

1 bulb fennel, quartered, cored, thinly sliced, tops removed and fronds reserved for garnish

2 teaspoons minced garlic

8 cups chicken broth

2 boneless, skinless chicken breasts (8 ounces *each*)

2 carrots, peeled and thinly sliced

2 sprigs fresh thyme

1 whole bay leaf

Salt and black pepper

½ cup uncooked orzo

1. Heat oil in large skillet over medium heat. Add onion and sliced fennel; cook 8 minutes or until tender. Add garlic; cook and stir 1 minute. Remove to **CROCK-POT**® slow cooker. Add broth, chicken, carrots, thyme, bay leaf, salt and pepper. Cover; cook on HIGH 2 to 3 hours.

2. Remove chicken to large cutting board; shred with two forks. Add orzo to **CROCK-POT**® slow cooker. Cover; cook on HIGH 30 minutes. Stir shredded chicken back into **CROCK-POT**® slow cooker. Remove and discard thyme sprigs and bay leaf. Garnish each serving with fennel fronds.

MAKES 6 TO 8 SERVINGS

CANNELLINI MINESTRONE SOUP

4 cups chicken broth

2 cups escarole, cut into ribbons

1 can (about 14 ounces) diced tomatoes

1 can (12 ounces) tomato-vegetable juice

1 cup chopped green onions

1 cup chopped carrots

1 cup chopped celery

1 cup chopped potatoes

¼ cup dried cannellini beans, rinsed and sorted

2 tablespoons chopped fresh chives

1 tablespoon chopped fresh Italian parsley

¼ teaspoon salt

¼ teaspoon black pepper

2 ounces uncooked ditalini pasta

1. Combine broth, escarole, tomatoes, vegetable juice, green onions, carrots, celery, potatoes, beans, chives, parsley, salt and pepper in **CROCK-POT®** slow cooker; stir to blend. Cover; cook on LOW 6 to 8 hours or on HIGH 4 to 6 hours.

2. Stir in pasta. Cover; cook on HIGH 20 minutes or until pasta is tender.

MAKES 6 SERVINGS

ITALIAN HILLSIDE GARDEN SOUP

1 tablespoon olive oil

1 cup chopped green bell pepper

1 cup chopped onion

½ cup sliced celery

1 can (about 14 ounces) diced tomatoes with basil, garlic and oregano

1 can (about 15 ounces) navy beans, rinsed and drained

1 medium zucchini, chopped

1 cup frozen cut green beans

2 cans (about 14 ounces *each*) chicken broth

¼ teaspoon garlic powder

1 package (9 ounces) refrigerated sausage- or cheese-filled tortellini pasta

3 tablespoons chopped fresh basil

Grated Asiago or Parmesan cheese (optional)

1. Heat oil in large skillet over medium-high heat. Add bell pepper, onion and celery; cook and stir 4 minutes or until onion is translucent. Remove to **CROCK-POT**® slow cooker.

2. Add tomatoes, navy beans, zucchini, green beans, broth and garlic powder. Cover; cook on LOW 7 hours or on HIGH 3½ hours.

3. Add tortellini. Cover; cook on HIGH 20 to 25 minutes or until pasta is tender. Stir in basil. Garnish with cheese.

MAKES 6 SERVINGS

POTATO CHEDDAR SOUP

2 pounds new red potatoes,
   cut into ½-inch cubes

3 cups vegetable broth

¾ cup coarsely chopped carrots

1 medium onion, coarsely
   chopped

½ teaspoon salt

1 cup half-and-half

¼ teaspoon black pepper

2 cups (8 ounces) shredded
   Cheddar cheese

1. Place potatoes, broth, carrots, onion and salt in **CROCK-POT**® slow cooker. Cover; cook on LOW 6 to 7 hours or on HIGH 3 to 3½ hours or until vegetables are tender.

2. Stir in half-and-half and pepper. Cover; cook on HIGH 15 minutes. Turn off heat. Remove lid; let stand 5 minutes. Stir in cheese until melted.

MAKES 6 SERVINGS

RICH AND HEARTY DRUMSTICK SOUP

2 turkey drumsticks (about 1¾ pounds *total*)

4½ cups chicken broth

2 medium carrots, sliced

1 medium stalk celery, thinly sliced

1 cup chopped onion

1 teaspoon minced garlic

½ teaspoon poultry seasoning

2 ounces uncooked egg noodles

¼ cup chopped fresh Italian parsley

2 tablespoons butter

¾ teaspoon salt

1. Coat inside of **CROCK-POT**® slow cooker with nonstick cooking spray. Add turkey, broth, carrots, celery, onion, garlic and poultry seasoning. Cover; cook on HIGH 5 hours.

2. Remove turkey to large cutting board. Add noodles to **CROCK-POT**® slow cooker. Cover; cook on HIGH 30 minutes or until noodles are tender.

3. Meanwhile, cut turkey into 1-inch pieces; discard bones. Stir turkey, parsley, butter and salt into **CROCK-POT**® slow cooker. Cover; cook on HIGH 10 minutes or until heated through.

MAKES 4 SERVINGS

CHICKEN TORTILLA SOUP

2 cans (about 14 ounces *each*) diced tomatoes

1 can (4 ounces) diced mild green chiles, drained

1 cup chicken broth, divided

1 yellow onion, diced

2 cloves garlic, minced

1 teaspoon ground cumin

4 boneless, skinless chicken thighs

Salt and black pepper

4 corn tortillas, sliced into ¼-inch strips

2 tablespoons chopped fresh cilantro

½ cup (2 ounces) shredded Monterey Jack cheese

1 avocado, diced and tossed with lime juice

Lime wedges

1. Combine tomatoes, chiles, ½ cup broth, onion, garlic and cumin in **CROCK-POT**® slow cooker; stir to blend. Add chicken. Cover; cook on LOW 6 hours or on HIGH 3 hours.

2. Remove chicken to large cutting board; shred with two forks. Stir shredded chicken, salt, pepper and additional ½ cup broth, if necessary, into **CROCK-POT**® slow cooker.

3. Just before serving, add tortillas and cilantro to **CROCK-POT**® slow cooker; stir to blend. Top each serving with cheese, avocado and squeeze of lime juice.

MAKES 4 TO 6 SERVINGS

PUMPKIN SOUP WITH CRUMBLED BACON AND TOASTED PUMPKIN SEEDS

2 teaspoons olive oil

½ cup raw pumpkin seeds*

3 slices thick-cut bacon

1 medium onion, chopped

1 teaspoon kosher salt

½ teaspoon chipotle chili powder

½ teaspoon black pepper

2 cans (29 ounces *each*) 100% pumpkin purée

4 cups chicken broth

¾ cup apple cider

½ cup whipping cream or half-and-half

Sour cream (optional)

Raw pumpkin seeds or pepitas may be found in the produce or ethnic food section of your local supermarket.

1. Coat inside of **CROCK-POT®** slow cooker with nonstick cooking spray. Heat oil in small skillet over medium-high heat. Add pumpkin seeds; cook and stir about 1 minute or until seeds begin to pop. Spoon into small bowl; set aside.

2. Add bacon to skillet; cook and stir until crisp. Remove bacon to paper towel-lined plate using slotted spoon. Reserve drippings in skillet. Crumble bacon when cool enough to handle; set aside.

3. Reduce heat to medium. Add onion to skillet; cook 3 minutes or until translucent. Stir in salt, chipotle chili powder and pepper. Remove onion mixture to **CROCK-POT®** slow cooker.

4. Whisk pumpkin purée, broth and cider into **CROCK-POT®** slow cooker until smooth. Cover; cook on HIGH 4 hours.

5. Turn off heat; remove lid. Whisk in cream. Adjust seasonings as necessary. Strain soup into bowls; garnish with pumpkin seeds, bacon and sour cream.

MAKES 4 SERVINGS

CAULIFLOWER SOUP

2 heads cauliflower,
   cut into small florets

8 cups chicken broth

¾ cup chopped celery

¾ cup chopped onion

2 teaspoons salt

2 teaspoons black pepper

2 cups milk or whipping cream

1 teaspoon Worcestershire sauce

1. Combine cauliflower, broth, celery, onion, salt and pepper in **CROCK-POT®** slow cooker. Cover; cook on LOW 7 to 8 hours or on HIGH 3 to 4 hours.

2. Pour cauliflower mixture into food processor or blender; process until smooth. Add milk and Worcestershire sauce; process until blended. Pour soup back into **CROCK-POT®** slow cooker. Cover; cook on HIGH 15 to 20 minutes or until heated through.

MAKES 8 SERVINGS

PLANTATION PEANUT SOUP

6 cups chicken broth

2 cups whipping cream

1 cup chunky peanut butter

1 cup chopped peanuts, divided

½ cup chopped onion

½ cup chopped celery

4 tablespoons (½ stick) butter

½ teaspoon salt

½ cup water

½ cup all-purpose flour

1. Combine broth, cream, peanut butter, ½ cup peanuts, onion, celery, butter and salt in **CROCK-POT**® slow cooker. Cover; cook on LOW 4 hours.

2. Turn **CROCK-POT**® slow cooker to HIGH. Stir water into flour in small bowl until smooth; whisk into soup. Cover; cook on HIGH 20 to 25 minutes or until thickened, stirring occasionally. Garnish with remaining ½ cup peanuts.

MAKES 8 SERVINGS

VEGETABLE SOUP WITH BEANS

4 cups vegetable broth

1 can (about 15 ounces) cannellini beans, rinsed and drained

1 can (about 14 ounces) diced tomatoes

16 baby carrots

1 medium onion, chopped

1 ounce dried oyster mushrooms, chopped

3 tablespoons tomato paste

2 teaspoons garlic powder

1 teaspoon dried basil

1 teaspoon dried oregano

½ teaspoon dried rosemary

½ teaspoon dried marjoram

½ teaspoon dried sage

½ teaspoon dried thyme

¼ teaspoon black pepper

French bread slices, toasted (optional)

1. Combine broth, beans, tomatoes, carrots, onion, mushrooms, tomato paste, garlic powder, basil, oregano, rosemary, marjoram, sage, thyme and pepper in **CROCK-POT**® slow cooker; stir to blend.

2. Cover; cook on LOW 8 hours or on HIGH 4 to 5 hours. Serve with bread, if desired.

MAKES 6 SERVINGS

SIMMERED SPLIT PEA SOUP

3 cans (about 14 ounces *each*) chicken broth

1 package (16 ounces) dried split peas, rinsed and sorted

8 slices bacon, crisp-cooked, chopped and divided

1 onion, chopped

2 carrots, chopped

1 teaspoon black pepper

½ teaspoon dried thyme

1 whole bay leaf

Combine broth, peas, half of bacon, onion, carrots, pepper, thyme and bay leaf in **CROCK-POT**® slow cooker. Cover; cook on LOW 6 to 8 hours. Remove and discard bay leaf. Garnish with remaining half of bacon.

MAKES 6 SERVINGS

BROCCOLI CHEDDAR SOUP

3 tablespoons butter

1 medium onion, chopped

3 tablespoons all-purpose flour

¼ teaspoon ground nutmeg

¼ teaspoon black pepper

4 cups vegetable broth

1 large bunch broccoli, chopped

1 medium red potato, peeled and chopped

1 teaspoon salt

1 whole bay leaf

1½ cups (6 ounces) shredded Cheddar cheese, plus additional for garnish

½ cup whipping cream

1. Melt butter in medium saucepan over medium heat. Add onion; cook and stir 6 minutes or until softened. Add flour, nutmeg and pepper; cook and stir 1 minute. Remove to **CROCK-POT**® slow cooker. Stir in broth, broccoli, potato, salt and bay leaf.

2. Cover; cook on HIGH 3 hours. Remove and discard bay leaf. Add soup in batches to food processor or blender; purée until desired consistency. Pour soup back into **CROCK-POT**® slow cooker. Stir in 1½ cups cheese and cream until cheese is melted. Garnish with additional cheese.

MAKES 6 SERVINGS

CHICKEN RAMEN NOODLE BOWLS

1 tablespoon olive oil

1 pound boneless, skinless chicken thighs

1 large yellow onion, peeled and halved

6 cups chicken broth

2 tablespoons soy sauce

4 green onions, divided

1 (1-inch) piece fresh ginger, sliced

1 clove garlic

6 ounces shiitake mushrooms, thinly sliced

⅓ cup hoisin sauce

8 ounces uncooked fresh ramen noodles

3 hard-cooked eggs, cut in half lengthwise

¼ cup thinly sliced red bell pepper

Fresh cilantro leaves

1. Heat oil in large skillet over medium-high heat. Add chicken; cook 8 to 10 minutes or until browned. Remove chicken to **CROCK-POT**® slow cooker using slotted spoon. Add onion halves to skillet, cut side down; cook 4 to 5 minutes or until lightly charred. Remove onion halves to **CROCK-POT**® slow cooker. Add broth, soy sauce, 2 green onions, ginger and garlic.

2. Cover; cook on LOW 6 to 7 hours or on HIGH 3 to 4 hours. Remove chicken to large cutting board; shred with two forks. Strain broth into large bowl. Discard solids; return broth to **CROCK-POT**® slow cooker. Stir in mushrooms and hoisin sauce. Cover; cook on HIGH 30 minutes.

3. Divide noodles and broth evenly among six bowls. Top each bowl evenly with chicken, mushrooms, one egg half, bell pepper and cilantro. Chop remaining 2 green onions; sprinkle evenly over bowls.

MAKES 6 SERVINGS

VOLUME MEASUREMENTS (dry)

$1/8$ teaspoon = 0.5 mL
$1/4$ teaspoon = 1 mL
$1/2$ teaspoon = 2 mL
$3/4$ teaspoon = 4 mL
1 teaspoon = 5 mL
1 tablespoon = 15 mL
2 tablespoons = 30 mL
$1/4$ cup = 60 mL
$1/3$ cup = 75 mL
$1/2$ cup = 125 mL
$2/3$ cup = 150 mL
$3/4$ cup = 175 mL
1 cup = 250 mL
2 cups = 1 pint = 500 mL
3 cups = 750 mL
4 cups = 1 quart = 1 L

VOLUME MEASUREMENTS (fluid)

1 fluid ounce (2 tablespoons) = 30 mL
4 fluid ounces ($1/2$ cup) = 125 mL
8 fluid ounces (1 cup) = 250 mL
12 fluid ounces ($1 1/2$ cups) = 375 mL
16 fluid ounces (2 cups) = 500 mL

WEIGHTS (mass)

$1/2$ ounce = 15 g
1 ounce = 30 g
3 ounces = 90 g
4 ounces = 120 g
8 ounces = 225 g
10 ounces = 285 g
12 ounces = 360 g
16 ounces = 1 pound = 450 g

DIMENSIONS

$1/16$ inch = 2 mm
$1/8$ inch = 3 mm
$1/4$ inch = 6 mm
$1/2$ inch = 1.5 cm
$3/4$ inch = 2 cm
1 inch = 2.5 cm

OVEN TEMPERATURES

250°F = 120°C
275°F = 140°C
300°F = 150°C
325°F = 160°C
350°F = 180°C
375°F = 190°C
400°F = 200°C
425°F = 220°C
450°F = 230°C

BAKING PAN SIZES

Utensil	Size in Inches/Quarts	Metric Volume	Size in Centimeters
Baking or Cake Pan (square or rectangular)	$8 \times 8 \times 2$	2 L	$20 \times 20 \times 5$
	$9 \times 9 \times 2$	2.5 L	$23 \times 23 \times 5$
	$12 \times 8 \times 2$	3 L	$30 \times 20 \times 5$
	$13 \times 9 \times 2$	3.5 L	$33 \times 23 \times 5$
Loaf Pan	$8 \times 4 \times 3$	1.5 L	$20 \times 10 \times 7$
	$9 \times 5 \times 3$	2 L	$23 \times 13 \times 7$
Round Layer Cake Pan	$8 \times 1 1/2$	1.2 L	20×4
	$9 \times 1 1/2$	1.5 L	23×4
Pie Plate	$8 \times 1 1/4$	750 mL	20×3
	$9 \times 1 1/4$	1 L	23×3
Baking Dish or Casserole	1 quart	1 L	—
	$1 1/2$ quart	1.5 L	—
	2 quart	2 L	—